Advance praise for *The Spiritual Guidance of Children: Montessori, Godly Play, and the Future*

With help from the poets, Berryman opens us to the creative center of ourselves, that space where even adults may yet discover the graced mystery of the triune God. Count me as one of many apprentices awed by Berryman's spiritual mastery and life-long friendship with little ones who herald the Kingdom.

—Fred P. Edie, Associate Professor for the Practice
of Christian Education, Duke Divinity School;
Faculty Advisor, Duke Youth Academy for Christian Formation

There are layers and layers of meaning here, and this book is not merely one to be read but rather to be engaged as a catalyst—an extended meditation inviting substantive reflection by Christian educators, spiritual directors, pastoral counselors, preachers and congregational leaders alike.

—The Right Reverend Robert O'Neill, Bishop of Colorado

This book, so eloquently written, presents a detailed history of the theory and practice of *Godly Play*. But more importantly, within the pages of this text, Berryman playfully challenges us (as only he can) to place children at the centre of the church—to reorient the church around the mutual blessing of both children and adults. It deserves to be read by a wide audience.

—Dr. Brendan Hyde, Senior Lecturer in Religious Education,
Australian Catholic University

For anyone who has ever wondered about the back-story of *Godly Play*, about its Montessorian roots and its place in the history of Religious Education, *The Spiritual Guidance of Children* is the book to read. Jerome Berryman convincingly argues that childhood catechesis in the post-secular age must take the form of spiritual guidance. His observations of children absorbed in flow, play, love and contemplation have lead him to believe that a Church which dares to "follow the child" will find the strength and vision it needs to renew itself.

—Robert Hurley, Professor of New Testament Studies
and Catechetics, Laval University, Quebec City

Dr. Jerome Berryman asserts that children have the same "existential issues and fears" that we adults do, and that learning the "classic Christian language system" as children is key to successfully managing those issues and fears across the lifespan. He places *Godly Play* firmly in the center of the conversation about how best to instill the Christian language system in children, and by extension, make it all the more useful to their adult mentors and guides. He also asks the startling question: "What if the energy invested in seeking new adult church members were spent inviting children into the congregation with radical generosity and commensurate skill?

—John Chattin-McNichols, Ph.D. Associate Professor
of Education, Seattle University

Even in his early work in the 1970s, Jerome Berryman wrote with an authority and wisdom *far* ahead of his contemporaries. In this latest book, we are taken further still. Not only is this a first-class consolidation of his 40 years of insight and passion for a Christian approach to children's spiritual lives—*and* for evolving an authentically child-centred approach in the Church—this book also provides a most compelling and detailed manifesto for the challenges ahead.

—Rebecca Nye, PhD. Associate Lecturer, The Open
University, Cambridge, UK and Freelance Researcher
and Consultant in Children's Spirituality.

This richly documented book now gives us the context for the deep thinking and emotion present in the activity of *Godly Play* and introduces us to Berryman's underlying construct of the *middle realm*; akin to *Flow* and *Zen* that is an outcome of play and "doing *midrash*."

—Rabbi Dr. Michael Shire, Dean and Professor, Shoolman Graduate
School of Jewish Education, Hebrew College, Boston.

The Spiritual Guidance of Children

Montessori, Godly Play, and the Future

JEROME W. BERRYMAN

Morehouse Publishing
NEW YORK · HARRISBURG · DENVER

Morehouse Publishing, 4775 Linglestown Road, Harrisburg, PA 17112

Morehouse Publishing, 19 East 34th Street, New York, NY 10016

Morehouse Publishing is an imprint of Church Publishing Incorporated.
www.churchpublishing.org

Cover design by Laurie Klein Westhafer
Typeset by Rose Design

Library of Congress Cataloging-in-Publication Data

Berryman, Jerome.
The spiritual guidance of children : Montessori, Godly play, and the future / Jerome
W. Berryman.
    pages cm
Includes bibliographical references and index.
  ISBN 978-0-8192-2840-6 (pbk.)—ISBN 978-0-8192-2841-3 (ebook) 1. Play—
Religious aspects—Christianity. 2. Christian education—Teaching methods. 3. Christian
education—Philosophy. 4. Christian education of children. 5. Montessori method
of education. I. Title.
BV1536.3.B46 2013
268'.432—dc23

2013022645

Printed in the United States of America

To all the children
Thea and I
learned from
for so many decades,
and for Thea,
forever . . .

contents

preface

This book reframes "Christian education" for children as spiritual guidance. It explores how best to transfer the whole Christian language system, which implies a way of life and spiritual development, from one generation to another.

Everything we do with children in the church guides their spirituality, but in our time, learning *how to speak Christian* is a matter of great importance because Christian language is no longer widely or well spoken. It is meant to be used to make existential meaning, to find direction in life and death, and to celebrate what truly matters. If children can learn this language and its connotations of playful orthodoxy early, then, as with any language, they have a better chance to become fluent, which will contribute to their spiritual quest and flourishing. One needs to know the art of speaking Christian language well to know the art of living well.

The approach to spiritual guidance described here is Godly Play. It came from the tradition of Montessori religious education, which began in 1907 in Rome. From the beginning Maria Montessori was very interested in the spirituality of children and their teachers. When it comes to what one actually does in a Godly Play room there are many publications to introduce this, so the focus of this book is on a new question: How does Godly Play feel and why is that important?

The first chapter challenges the reader to think "bigger" about children's Christian education by reframing it as the mutual guidance of children and adults together. Chapters two and three tell the story of the tradition of Montessori religious education, because knowing where Godly Play has come from can help us know where it is going. Chapters four and five describe the "middle realm," which is how Godly Play feels when children are invited into the domain (the home) of classical Christian language to absorb and activate it to make existential meaning.

Godly Play feels like the creative process in action. To be more specific it feels like flow, play, love, and contemplation, which are the four dimensions of this process. These dimensions of the creative process share the same structure, so they appear to have differentiated from our fundamental human core. This center point, which we knew as a unity when we were infants, is not just something we do when we create new ideas. It is who we are psychologically, socially, biologically, and spiritually and it is how we know ourselves as well as God.

This kind of guidance follows Jesus' counsel that in order to be spiritually mature, we need to become like children and to become like children we need to welcome them, which in turn reveals him and the one who sent him. The language of the Christian people flows out of Jesus' life and words, so it makes sense that this language can be used to guide us back to our source as well as toward our ending.

The last chapter shows how Godly Play's approach to spiritual guidance has become diffused into the mainstream of Christian education and has been applied in a variety of different situations. When this diffusion and adaptation is combined with clarity about Godly Play's identity a milieu is created in which further exploration can flourish to find better ways for the mutual blessing of children and adults to guide Godly Play and the church into the future.

acknowledgments

Thea is in every page of this book. She knew many of the people mentioned here and we especially loved our trips to Rome, sometimes with our girls and sometimes alone, to visit Sofia. It does not seem possible that Thea died in 2009, but this book is a kind of birthday present to her. Our girls Alyda and Coleen are also part of this book, as always, but this time Coleen especially thought her Dad would never be done. She witnessed so many revisions that the birth of an actual book seemed unimaginable.

My mentors, Professor Cam Wyckoff at Princeton Theological Seminary and Professoressa Sofia Cavalletti in Rome, supported *something*, when no one knew what it was! Their extravagant generosity and energy was given for itself, a true act of play and blessing. What they helped begin, children have led the way to continue.

Zoe Cole, who helped with the book, considered it strong enough to support by challenging every idea, every chapter, every sentence, and every footnote. Her attention to detail and broad background as a lawyer, a teacher of adults and children, and her work on her Ph.D. at the University of Denver in philosophy, theology, and political thought made her a wonderful conversation partner to move the book along to its completion.

The people at Venice, a superb Italian restaurant nearby, helped more than they may realize. Alessandro Carollo, Christian Della Fave, and Gabriel Aragon created the cuisine for writing and thinking while Nunzio Marino presided over the dining room to make it a graceful place. Rachid, Victor, and Leticcia also deserve special mention.

Finally, Jim Wahler, my editor at Church Publishing, patiently and creatively pulled this project together to give shape to it sprawling ideas so you can now hold it in your hands to weigh its worth. His editorial skill was as important as his ability to keep the project moving. Dirk DeVries, Robin Lybeck, and others at Church Publishing in Denver have been in the background cheering. Their encouragement has been important. Ryan Masteller finished the final editing with competent alacrity and Davis Perkins, the publisher of CPI in New York City, played his part well, as always, for which I continue to be deeply grateful.

Jerome W. Berryman
Denver, Colorado
February 4, 2013

1.

Children and the Quest for Spiritual Maturity

What do children need from adults and what do adults need from children for the spiritual quest? The answer is the same for both: spiritual guidance. Children require adult spiritual guidance, because they need the permission and the means to develop their spirituality. Adults require children's spiritual guidance, because by being who they are, children can refresh and re-center spiritual growth in adults. Without this mutual blessing children and adults are likely to lack the dynamic wholeness and authenticity they were created to enjoy.

What are the means for spiritual guidance? They are the same for children and adults. They come in a toolbox called "classical, Christian language." Children need to begin learning the art of how to use these tools as early as possible to live meaningfully within the existential edges of their being and knowing. Adults need to continue developing this art by renewing what they knew as children of God's presence, so they can think about what this means for their daily lives in richer and more flexible ways.

The phrase "classical, Christian language" may be offensive to some. It sounds pretentious and overbearing. The phrase feels historically stuck. It snarls and can signify dysfunction. I understand these connotations because I have felt them myself. Still, be patient. Relax. Enjoy the story. It's about crawling out on a limb.

---------------------------- * ----------------------------

When I was a child we lived in a brown house on a corner. I could look out of my bedroom window and see my grandmother's white house on the other corner. Between us was her overflowing flower garden. Across the street I could see the playground of the grade school where I spent eight years and just beyond grandmother's corner was the solid brick church with its square bell tower. Not every child gets to grow up with such a correlation of space and destiny or the safety and freedom to explore it.

One summer evening I was listening to the grown-ups talking on my grandmother's porch while I was catching lightning bugs in the twilight. Someone said, "He'd crawled out too far," and everyone laughed. I moved closer and asked, "What's 'too far'?"

"Oh, you know, when the limb breaks off."

"How do you know when that's going to happen?"

"You just do."

"What happens then?"

"You fall." Everyone laughed again.

"What happens then?"

"Go run and play." I did, but the next day I began to look at the trees in my grandmother's yard in a different way.

Then it happened. I climbed up into a large apricot tree and crawled slowly out on a limb, farther and farther and farther.

It began to bend. I didn't hear the sound, like a big stick breaking, until I was on my back in the grass looking up. I was lying amid ripe apricots with the splintered limb beside me. We—the limb, the apricots and I—had all fallen. I can still smell the rotting fruit and hear the buzzing insects. Were they laughing? I was!

---✻---

The tree this book explores is about Godly Play, a well-developed way to provide spiritual guidance for children and adults *together*. Its goal is for children to enter adolescence with an inner working model of the Christian language system. By a "working model" I mean the ability to use classical Christian language to create meaning about life and death. Since about 1984, Godly Players have thought about this goal in terms of "speaking Christian" as a second language.

"Speaking Christian" as a Second Language

If "speaking Christian" is a second language, what is the first one? It is the language of everyday, which is a loose collection of phrases from technical languages such as engineering, physics, medicine, psychology, and law combined with regional and family colloquialisms.

We usually think of a "second language" as a foreign language, such as Spanish or German. In those cases we are aware that we need to get the words and gestures right to communicate. We also understand that knowing the cultural context is fundamental to understanding the meaning of the words. The same is true for specialized languages within English, such as law or medicine. Each has its technical vocabulary, gestures, and a cultural context. It may take years of graduate training to learn to speak such languages. Speaking Christian is also a specialized language within English, but its "foreignness" often goes unnoticed or underappreciated.

Learning "Christian" as a second language is more complex than often realized, because the language system is so odd. Its toolbox contains sacred stories, parables, liturgical *action*, and contemplative *silence*. Each of these four genres requires a different skill, awareness of tone, and a special art for using its form and content to make meaning.

Learning how to use this odd language is like learning any art. For example, how does one learn to be a painter? Can you learn this art by selling paintings, studying art history, manufacturing paintbrushes or paints, being the curator of an art museum, or knowing painters socially? No. To be a painter you need to paint. The same is true for the art of speaking Christian. You have to use it to know it and the earlier you begin to know it, the easier it is to become fluent, as with any language. Godly Play helps children learn this art early, so they can become artists of the Christian life.

The way Godly Play contributes to this art is by helping children associate Christian language with the creative process while they are using it to make existential meaning. This grounds them in their tradition and yet leaves them creatively open to explore the world with a kind of playful orthodoxy. This phrase, *playful orthodoxy*, sounds like an oxymoron only because *orthodoxy* and *play* are seldom associated. *Orthodoxy* usually stands for closure and *playful* nods toward openness. Together, however, they provide a safe place to venture out from and return to with the passion to know new people and ideas, as well as to meet the future in creative ways. Helping children get a feel for playful orthodoxy, as they learn to speak Christian, is more important than one might think, because

Christian language needs to be absorbed and activated by the whole person, since our existential limits involve every bit of who we are. This is why Christian education is bigger than you may think.

Christian Education Is Bigger Than You Think

Teaching a *specific* religion to children today is sometimes quietly dismissed or loudly rejected, but this response is largely irrational. It comes from thinking too small about Christian education. There are at least seven reasons for this. Most people, growing up inside or outside the church, have never experienced Christian education's comprehensive wholeness, which is more like spiritual *guidance* than *education* in the narrow sense.

First, most people don't usually realize that Christian education's larger vision involves communicating with and caring for the wholeness of the child's body-mind-spirit unity. When the body and spirit are ignored you get Christian education reduced to memory, reason, and will. The teaching becomes a transfer of church "facts," the telling and memorizing of Bible stories in clever ways, or learning reasons to believe. When the mind and spirit are trimmed away the result is adult-created art projects for children to copy, activity-as-entertainment, and force fed, high-energy games to keep children busy and out of the way. When spirituality is ignored, religion is taught as an empty practice, which is fruitless and obnoxious. When any truncated version of Christian education is substituted for the larger vision, then the teaching and learning loses touch with the existential reality of the children's lives.

Gabriel Moran, the great Roman Catholic educator, theologian, and linguistic philosopher began teaching and reflecting on teaching religion in 1958. After about forty years of experience he reduced what he was doing to two words in the title of his book, *Showing How*.[1] You probably already agree with him. Have you ever said ironically, "Do as I *say* but not as I do," and then laughed? The laughter shows that you already know that Christian education is about "showing how," rather than *talking* about something the children are supposed to think, feel, or do. It takes the whole person to show how the whole person is involved in the Christian life. This is why showing how is more important than explaining how in Christian education.

Christian education is also larger than commonly thought because it involves children in absorbing and activating the whole Christian language domain. This immensity is missed, because many adults are unclear themselves about the scope of Christian language as a system and the uniqueness of how its sacred stories, parables, liturgical action, and contemplative silence are integrated into a way of speaking and living. Some adults have also not realized that the primary function of this language domain is to make *existential* meaning, which is to think personally about who we truly are and the limits to our being and knowing. This may sound boring, but children are very happy to have a way to cope with their existential limits.

It is sometimes thought that children are not aware of their existential limits, so it is assumed that they would not be interested in learning how to cope with them, but that is an adult fallacy—one that results in the repression of childhood memories and gives too much credence to adult language and routine. Children grow so fast and experience so much chaos that they are always in touch with their limits. This is why Christian language is important to children and makes them happy to find adults who will help them cope with their boundaries by giving them this language.

The third reason many think too small about Christian education is to hide rather than celebrate God's vastness. Since God's presence is overwhelming, we often try to reduce God to something more manageable than infinity to teach.

In the middle of the last century when Christianity was supposedly in its modern ascendency, J. B. Phillips, a biblical scholar and theologian, published a little book with a big challenge: *Your God Is Too Small*.[2] He described thirteen small gods, which often masquerade as the God of Christianity. They are: the "Resident Policeman," "Parental Hangover," "Grand Old Man," "Meek-and-Mild," "Absolute Perfection," "Heavenly Bosom," "God-in-a-Box," "Managing Director," "Second-hand God," "Perennial Grievance," "Pale Galilean," "Projected Image," and "Assorted." He concluded that there must be more than elusive sparks and flashes of the divine when one takes seriously what might happen if God really did enter life on our planet. How would that work? Would not God need to be completely divine and completely human at the same time? But that's impossible, isn't it? It is only impossible if your thinking about God is too small. Christian education is about the big God.

A fourth way people try to shrink Christian education is by sending children off to be "educated" instead of being involved in the whole church. What if the energy invested in seeking new adult members were spent inviting children into the congregation with radical generosity and skill? Much of the decline in church membership comes from children leaving and not coming back. Perhaps, if we provided something useful for the development of their spirituality and they were part of the community, then they would remain. Of course, they would critique what is going on from their generation's point of view, but they would do this as insiders rather than outsiders, which is what the church needs.

Excluding children from the congregation can be obvious as well as subtle. Obvious ways have been catalogued many times, but a more *subtle exclusion is to not teach Christian language* to children so they can speak the language of their community! When teaching Christian language fails, exclusion is taught by default. Children may even be included politically in the church but if they are not included spiritually and linguistically they are not full members.

Ignoring children in the church is an unrealized defensive act. Children present a powerful challenge to what adults conceive of as spiritual maturity. Jesus was very forthright when speaking about this error, made by his disciples, as well as us. He said that if you want to become spiritually mature you need to become like a child (Matthew 18:3, Mark 10:15, Luke 18:17) and if you really want to know him and the one who sent him, you need to welcome children (Mark 9:37). His seriousness about this was expressed in the millstone texts, which were also recorded in all three synoptic gospels (Matthew 18:6, Mark 9:42, Luke 17:2).

The power of becoming like children and welcoming them cannot be understood if it is not experienced, but it can't be experienced if adults avoid being with children in the church. If Jesus' disciples didn't understand this, why should we expect people to "get it" today? One reason we should expect more from adults today is that we have a more open view of children in our society than the disciples did in the first century. This is often blocked, however, *in the church* by the *de facto* theology of children, which still functions informally. We have an unspoken theological heritage of ambivalence, ambiguity, and indifference toward children that still outweighs our understanding of children as a means of grace.[3]

A fifth reason we think too small about Christian education is that we underestimate the role it plays in the constructive communication *among all the world's religions*. This lack of appreciation is changing,[4] but Christians need a deep and solid, yet open and creative appropriation of their own *language and way of life* to be able to talk with people of other religions from depth to depth. This is of growing importance because the people from other religions, who used to live across the oceans, now live across the street. It is sobering to ask what we are teaching about Christianity by the way we live our daily lives and the language we use to talk about life and death.

Communicating from depth to depth is not just a matter of communicating what Christianity is. It is also about putting ourselves in the shoes of people from other religions, but this is impossible if we have never mindfully experienced walking in our own shoes as Christians. One needs to know the pinching limits and the expansive beauty of our own shoes to fully appreciate what it is like to walk in the shoes of others.

Communicating from depth to depth is the only way to build trust, despite difference, that is strong enough to deal with the stress and strain caused by the violent aberrations found in all religions. Communicating from depth to depth with perspective is how the religions of the world can become the solution for violence rather than its cause. This large and noble calling for Christian education goes far beyond fomenting suspicion or advocating for blandness as the only alternatives to religious differences. It challenges us to move forward with people of other religions to help heal the earth.

There is a sixth way that Christian education has been diminished. This has to do with gender. Children need to experience men and women working *together* with them in Christian education. Christianity is not about being male or female. It is about working and praying together regardless of differences. Most Christian educators know and deeply care that an all-female church school teaches something they don't mean to teach.

I can't help but smile as I write this. Thea and I worked together in Presbyterian and Episcopal parishes for nearly fifty years. The roles associated with males and females were always being challenged back and forth between us and with the parish. There was laughter, seriousness, frustration, teasing, and uproarious satire. Still, it was only occasionally that we were able to satisfy our ideal of a man and woman working together, as we did, in each Godly Play room. Teaching such wholeness is not just a matter for the church but it is important for the future health of our species.

Finally, Christian education is reduced when it does not help enrich the wholeness of our species. The wholeness I am referring to is not just about being male and female. It is about the millions of years it took to develop a brain big enough to support the kind of thinking we take for granted today and the social patterns needed to support infants, during their long apprenticeship compared with other species, to become human. This all came together about thirty thousand years ago to produce a human being,[5] but today we are in danger of shrinking our view of humankind when we take too small a view of Christian education.

Steven Mithen combined knowledge about prehistory with modern cognitive science to stake out a theory about our humanity. First, our ancestors had minds dominated by a general intelligence. Second, their general intelligence divided into specialized intelligences, like the blades of a Swiss army knife.[6] Finally, cognitive fluidity developed to the point that the special intelligences could work together. Art, religion, and science (making and using tools) began to blend to create the modern mind.[7]

Here is where Christian education comes into play. Our ability to blend art, religion, and science is being challenged today by new kinds of rigidity. The abstract mind is being expanded electronically at the expense of face-to-face communication. Modern multi-tasking moves us toward thinking in modules like a Swiss army knife. The struggle with information overload overwhelms us and causes chronic reductionism, so we tend to think in bumper stickers and sound bites. Finally, there is the temptation to diminish religious experience and beauty in favor of a dominating hyper-module for science. These four tendencies toward rigidity reduce our cognitive fluidity, which fractures the wholeness of what it means to be human. If Christian education emphasizes the fluidity of children's thinking in art, religion, and science, then it can contribute to children being more human than Neanderthal and place Christian education at the leading edge of human development.

If Christian education is larger and more expansive than we have previously imagined, then we need to be especially careful about shrinking it down to irrelevance. Still, the Sunday school has a long and distinguished history, so we need to know where it has come from to know where we should go from here.

The Sunday School Movement and Its Critics

The Sunday school movement began as a project to help prevent children in the English slums from falling into a life of crime because of neglect and illiteracy. Additional motivations were to protect the Sabbath from misuse and property from destruction on the only day of the week when children were not working at such tasks as sweeping chimneys, toiling in the mills and mines, bottling and labeling boot black, or mass-producing pins by hand. The goals of literacy, moral development, and

Christian evangelism converged to find a way to bring young people into churches to worship on Sunday and learn how to read the Bible to improve their lives.

Newspaper editor Robert Raikes is often credited as one of the founders of the Sunday school. He lived in Gloucester, near the English border with Wales and his first school opened in Sooty Alley in 1780 over the objections of various groups, including the Archbishop of Canterbury. He experimented for three years with poor children from the factory districts and then published the results in his own newspaper, the *Gloucester Journal* on November 3, 1783.

Raikes wrote that the "lawless state of the younger class" was curbed and "where this plan has been adopted, we are assured that the behavior of the children is greatly civilized." Children learned how to read in Sunday school but not always to write because of a fierce debate about whether writing was a proper activity for the Lord's Day. They also memorized a catechism and attended worship.

Discipline was strict for these children from six to fourteen years of age. "Some were hobbled with heavy weights, logs, or shackles bound to their ankles."[8] Nevertheless, some, like Charles Shaw, remembered this experience as "an oasis in the desert to me," as he wrote in his memoir of an impoverished childhood in the Potteries during the 1830s.[9]

John L. Elias, a longtime professor at Fordham University, traced the growth of the Sunday school from the late eighteenth century to today by saying, "It went from being a school for the poor and working classes to an instrument of evangelical or revivalist Protestantism to what it is today, a school for the education of Protestant believers of all ages."[10] While the Protestant approach was usually located in the local church, the Roman Catholics set up a parallel school system in the United

States. It was often organized around ethnic parishes, to serve the many Roman Catholic immigrants arriving from Europe during the nineteenth century. Both strategies used teacher-focused authority and instruction as their tour de force.

Sunday schools spread in the United States as well as in England. The non-denominational and evangelical American Sunday School Union was formed in 1824 in Philadelphia and swept across the country, even sending missionaries to other countries. Another example from a very different theological orientation was the Sunday School Society. Its origin was in "Sabbath" schools set up by Unitarian ministers in Boston. By 1831 it too had spread across the country.

Despite the success of the Sunday school movement, it also had its critics. In 1837 at a meeting of the Sunday School Society William Channing, a Unitarian minister, "criticized the Sunday schools for their mechanical teaching and lifeless way they handed on the faith."[11] Channing was speaking to his fellow Unitarians when he expressed his concern that this approach was "stamping our minds on the young, making them see with our eyes, giving them information, burdening their memories, imposing outward behavior, rules and prejudices."[12]

Negative responses were also aroused when African Americans learned how to read in Sunday schools. Following Nat Turner's 1831 slave rebellion in Virginia, many southern states prohibited the education of slaves and free blacks. It was rumored that Nat Turner (1800–1831) had learned to read in a Sunday school, although his autobiography, *The Confessions of Nat Turner*, did not mention this. The reality was that most Sunday schools were white and ignored the reality of slavery.

Perhaps the best way to sense the milieu of the nineteenth-century Sunday school is to remember that Charles Dickens (1812–1870) published *A Christmas Carol* in 1843. His father was in debtors prison and Dickens himself worked ten-hour days as a child pasting labels on pots of boot black. The sadistic brutality of life as an apprentice and in schools runs like a river through his novels, such as *Oliver Twist*, *Nicholas Nickleby*, *David Copperfield*, and *Great Expectations*. Many poor children knew little more than neglect and violence while the rich children were pampered and idealized.

One of the greatest paradoxes in the history of childhood appeared in England during the nineteenth century. Children were romanticized and at the same time seen as uncivilized savages. The poetry of William Wordsworth and such stories as *Peter Pan* and *Alice in Wonderland* glorified children, while in the mills and the mines they lived like animals and were thought of in those terms. By the beginning of the twentieth century, however, the view of children began to change in society and among educators both in England and the United States.

In the United States John Dewey published *The School and Society* in 1900. He advocated for children *interacting* with the curriculum. He wanted them to be at the dynamic center of their own learning rather than only receiving instruction. Dewey also wanted education to include teaching children how to assume responsibility in a democratic society and to become leaders, rather than only learning how to be submissive to authority.

In 1903 the Religious Education Association was founded to bring the latest ideas in education, such as Dewey's, to the task of religious education. As the twentieth century continued so did the Sunday school, albeit with a new professionalism, especially when it was integrated into the programs of the mainline denominations. Still, a joke that had circulated during the late nineteenth century was still told: "When is a school not a school? When it is a Sunday school."

By mid-century, Christianity was apparently flourishing in the cities, suburbs, and countryside following World War II. Still, there were unsettling comments about Sunday school. The February 11, 1957, copy of *Life* magazine called the Sunday school "the most wasted hour in the week" and published a long and thoughtful article by Wesley Shrader, Associate Professor of Pastoral Theology at Yale Divinity School. The nature and effectiveness of the Sunday school was a question that was still being treated seriously in the public media.

In the 1960s the "death of god" movement appeared, which raised serious questions about the efficacy of Christian education, whether the death-of-god theologians had been read or not. The April 8, 1966, cover of *Time* magazine asked the question, "Is God dead?" in red ink on a black background. The articles inside discussed how atheism was growing in the United States.

When the 1970s began, John Westerhoff challenged the church's practice of Christian education with his *Values for Tomorrow's Children*. By mid-decade he sharpened his critique of the Sunday school with *Will Our Children Have Faith?* This book hit a raw nerve. New editions were published in 2000 and 2012—this last volume including forty-five pages of commentary on the first two editions as well as updates for each chapter.[13]

Westerhoff was critical of the "schooling and instructional model" and proposed a broader vision of education that included children's immersion in the life of the parish rather than relying on an hour of instruction each Sunday. He also published his ideas about faith development growing like the rings of a tree. People began to talk about faith being "caught, not taught."[14] Westerhoff's view of "socialization" involved such things as sharing a tradition, involvement in liturgy, purposeful interactions among three generations, and acting in society for justice as a community. It also involved children moving through *affiliative, searching,* and *owned* stages of faith. Nevertheless, the instructional model, which was more familiar and specific about its goals and objectives, continued to dominate. The 1970s closed with people being more sensitive to the context within which the teaching took place, but old habits were hard to break.

As the 1980s began Westerhoff's socialization model was elaborated by adding a historical perspective in *A Faithful Church: Issues in the History of Catechesis.* This book was a collection of articles, written by historians of religious education, "to help contemporary Christians move from a school model of Christian formation to a fuller catechesis." Westerhoff and his co-author hoped that the sociological model for education would "be aided by a historical argument," because the school model was "actually a relative late-comer on the scene of socialization into the church."[15] The book also urged the use of the term *catechesis* instead of *education,* because historically catechesis "includes every aspect of the church's life."[16]

Despite the efforts of Westerhoff and others to reform Christian education, the Sunday school continued to meet at its regular time and in its customary ways, even though nationwide there was a general decline in attendance, as the Sunday holiday became more secular than religious in observance. This was despite tremendous energy being applied to the educational task by experienced and concerned Christian educators in the parish, including myself, and there were many local exceptions to this downward trend.

The church school ceased to be a matter of national media attention in the decades that followed. The decline of interest in the Sunday school was accompanied with a rise in interest about spirituality, unrelated to church programs. For Christian educators this raised a troubling question. Had the church been unintentionally teaching children the wrong lesson? Did the teaching and socialization models combine somehow in their actual practice to promote a hidden curriculum, which taught that spirituality has nothing to do with church? We may have been thinking too small for too long about what it means to transfer a whole language system and way of life from one generation to another!

An Alternative to the Schooling and Socialization Models

Attacking the Sunday school is easy. Most experienced Christian educators are more aware of the paradoxes and problems involved in their work than their critics. What is difficult to do, however, is to present a detailed alternative to the status quo with a method, curriculum, theoretical foundation, and history to deepen or even reframe the discussion about what is best for the spiritual quest of children.

Godly Play is an effort to provide a well-developed alternative to the schooling and socialization models in order to further the conversation about what is best for children and adults in the church. This alternative comes from a tradition outside the Sunday school movement, so it brings with it a different perspective. This alternative, like the Sunday school, has a history. It began in 1907 when Dr. Maria Montessori opened her first school in a Roman slum, four years after the Religious Education Association was founded in the United States. The story of four generations of this tradition will be told in the next two chapters with gratitude to show where Godly Play has come from and the complexity of its foundation.

In 2012 Diana Butler Bass looked back over the last few centuries of Christian history in the United States and argued that today we are experiencing "The Great Reversal."[17] It is a spiritual awakening like those that took place during the periods of 1730 to 1760, 1800 to 1830, and 1890 to 1920. The present awakening began in 1960 and still continues. It is longer in duration than previous periods and the experience of spirituality comes *before* commitment to religion. Often there is no interest in religion at all! Bass described the old process as believing-behaving-belonging, but today the steps in the process are belonging-behaving-believing. The experience of God and the action that flows out of that awareness come before and often instead of joining a church or believing in doctrines and creeds.

In 1960, right on time according to Bass's chronology, I found myself objecting strenuously to the believing-behaving-belonging approach being taught at Princeton Theological Seminary in the required Christian education class. Dr. D. Campbell Wyckoff arranged for me to take a tutorial with him instead of the class he taught. I will be eternally grateful for his understanding. I was experiencing a conflict that I could not articulate. In the tutorial he assigned me the task of writing my own theory of Christian education, which I am still working on today, over fifty years later.

It took another decade for me to discover a method to do what I had intuited needed to be done. This insight came as Thea and I watched our girls in a Montessori school. At the beginning of the twentieth century Maria Montessori had argued that children were inherently spiritual and trained her teachers to guide children's spirituality, which includes their educational drive, to fulfill itself in their lives.

If you ask a Montessori child, "Who taught you that?" she or he is likely to say, "I don't know. I guess I taught myself."

This approach encouraged self-direction rather than being other-directed, which made it especially appropriate to honor children's personal experience of God. Since one must die for oneself, learning to live well also needs to be personal. This approach to Christian education recognized that children have an "owned faith" from the beginning and supported a life long journey toward greater maturity based on this. The Montessori approach largely bypassed Westerhoff's "affiliative faith," living by the faith of other people, to encourage children's personal quest alongside adult mentors, teaching each other mutually across the generations.

I soon discovered that not everyone agreed that Montessori education was the solution to the church's education problems. Even the mention of the word *Montessori* was sometimes enough for me to be shown the door. There was an uneasy sense that something had been turned upside down in Montessori education, which made church leaders suspicious despite a great deal of talk in the church about child-centered education. There were also many practical concerns that looked insurmountable, all of which are still relevant today. Six of these perceived problems are still worrisome and deserve comment.

The first concern is that Godly Play is "too difficult." The children's mentors need to be well-trained, whether they are volunteers or not. Godly Play is also expensive, but I must add that this investment is for the long term. The expensive materials last at least twenty years and well-trained mentors don't burn out. Children's *spiritual guidance* is also considered too difficult to take responsibility for, because it requires more specific and personal responsibility than either the schooling or socialization models require. This is because more attuned care and consistency is needed for children to provide such guidance. They are more vulnerable when they open up to wondering about their existential issues, so they need a safe place to do this and well-prepared people to guide them. People who work with children need to be more responsible than those who work with adults. Adults should be able to compensate for the deficiencies of their teachers. Children absorb them.

Another kind of practical resistance comes from the seemingly compulsive attention in Godly Play to the details and beauty of the prepared environment for teaching and learning. This is very *Montessori*, as you will see in the next chapters, but this is a strange objection. Adults are fastidious, even combative, about caring for the space in which *they* worship, but the place where children learn to speak the language that enables them to worship with the community is often barren and neglected. It is used for many other kinds of activities, so the space does not feel like it is truly for children. Godly Play attempts to integrate what takes place in the church's worship with what happens in the church school. The same standard of care is assumed for both settings.

A third kind of concern is about what goes on in the Godly Play rooms. Some worry that this is some kind of cult. Parents don't want their children to become religious fanatics or bigots. What they don't realize is that Godly Play helps children become deeply grounded in classical Christian language *and at the same time* enables them to be more self-directed and creatively open in their spirituality to new ideas, new situations, new people, and the future. The goal is not to take over children's spirits, minds, or bodies, but to free them to move in an integrated way toward a constructive, self-directed, life-long growth in God and in the church community.

A fourth concern is the opposite of the fear that Godly Play is rigid and over-controlling. People worry that Godly Play is too open. It is considered a breeding ground for little heretics.

This is very unlikely, because the environment surrounding children in a developed Godly Play room places them physically, mindfully, emotionally, and spiritually in the center of the sacred stories, parables, and liturgical action materials of the Christian language system. Their absorption and activation of this language takes place within a space infused with the contemplative silence of the classical Christian tradition. The objects for the lessons come literally from the surrounding shelves and are returned to that context when the lesson is finished. Besides, Godly Play always invites God, verbally and nonverbally, to come join in the theological play. This means that the power of the whole Christian language system, the presence of the well-trained mentor, the wisdom of the community of children, and God's presence in the room make it a place for playful orthodoxy rather than casual heresy.

Godly Play also troubles people by placing a confusing emphasis on Christian language *as a means* rather than as an end in itself. The themes in Jewish and Christian theology about idolatry, blasphemy, and hypocrisy are taken seriously, so the *art of using* sacred stories, parables, liturgical action, and contemplative prayer to make existential meaning is what is taught. Memorization takes place, nevertheless, sometimes directed but mostly self-motivated. The words and actions of the four genres, then, are not memorized for themselves, as if they were magic, but because they are useful to make meaning. Such learning is very satisfying and makes children deeply happy.

When *content* is over-emphasized the lesson becomes distant or irrelevant history and the words are worshipped instead of God. When *process* is over-emphasized the deep grounding in the classical language gets lost in cartoons, sparkles, high-energy games, and other distractions. Godly Play emphasizes a balance of content and process that is unique for each child in the Montessori manner, so a class of twenty children becomes twenty classes of one as well as a community.

A final concern is sometimes more felt than named. Shifting to Godly Play encourages a shift in thinking about the place of children in the community of the church. This is probably the cause of the greatest *implicit* resistance. Sometimes Godly Play is tried, despite this unacknowledged resistance, but such trial runs are usually brief and half-hearted, so the project fails and the curriculum is blamed.

Godly Play comes and goes. Sometimes it starts up, fails, starts again years later, and fails again. God laughs and plays. Sometimes it also becomes a lasting tradition in churches, schools, hospitals, and other settings. Children have the same teachers and touch the same materials their brothers and sisters used. Perhaps, one day, *their* children will also find their way into Godly Play.

Godly Play is not meant to be the latest, greatest thing in Christian education. It is not good *because it is new*! It is meant for the long run. New mentors stand in for previous generations of guides while the Godly Play rooms and their process remain much the same but deepening in beauty and detail. Sometimes the latest, easiest, most media-savvy thing is not what is needed to build a foundation for life-long learning. An approach that involves the mutual blessing of children and adults in an oral tradition is probably a better way to transfer the whole Christian language domain and way of life from one generation to another.

This final concern about the danger of Godly Play reorienting the whole church deserves additional comment. The possibility that Godly Play will reshape the concerns of a parish, school, or other institution is real. Let's call this the "Copernican revolution problem."

A Copernican Revolution in the Church?

Placing children instead of adults at the center of the circling bodies in the church is as unthinkable in our time as the solar system was in Copernicus's (1473–1543) day. It is hard to imagine that children are teachers as well as learners, but even when this shift takes place, things will go on pretty much the same. The sun will still "come up" in the morning and "go down" at night in Christian education.

All the activities usually found in an excellent ministry with children and families will continue. Children's choirs will meet. There will be vacation Bible school. Children and families will engage in service projects, spring festivals, slightly silly plays and musicals about the Bible to laugh together, and visits will be made to other places of worship to compare them with their own. Preparations for Holy Baptism and receiving Holy Communion will proceed with customary care. Children will continue to help in worship as greeters and acolytes. They will help take up the collection and bring the gifts forward with the adult ushers. Visits to mothers and their newborn babies will be delighted in. Going to visit the sick and shut-ins will continue. There will be parties for parents, workshops about toys, community networking, and other relevant things to make life for families better. Retreats for children and parents (and grandparents) will continue. Older people will be borrowed as unofficial grandparents during church so children can sit with them at times as well as with their parents to the benefit of all.

The caring and careful creativity of Christian educators abounds! Their ability to keep in motion all the activities mentioned above *and even more* is impressive and sometimes downright miraculous. What Godly Play adds at the center of such a mix is a place where children can absorb and activate classical Christian language to give the rest of the ministry with children and families more depth and meaning.

To keep this new orientation from collapsing two questions need to be asked about every expenditure and program in the church: How will this action impact the spiritual guidance of children? How can children be involved in an appropriate way? Both questions are about children, but they also involve adults. They open up opportunities for adults to mature in their own spirituality by working with children and thinking more carefully about their place in the community.

Many adults won't like this re-centering or see its relevance. They are no more likely to look at the church in this way than the clergy were likely to look at the moon through a telescope in Copernicus's time. The moon was supposed to be perfect since it was closer to God than the earth, so if they saw imperfections on the moon, such as craters, they might become disoriented and disillusioned. They might even lose their faith. The re-centering of the church around the mutual blessing of children and adults may also reveal imperfections in the church that are disorienting and disillusioning, but such a shakeup can open up more flexible and creative ways to think about how and why one is involved in the church's community.

Copernicus's revolution was so fundamental that it changed the way words were used, so we can expect that the re-centering of the church will do the same. Who will really want to say "the spiritual guidance of children" instead of "Sunday school"? It is an awkward phrase without alliteration, but beyond the words this implies taking responsibility for mentoring children's spirituality for their life-long learning. Seeing the church as a womb in which the spirituality of mutual blessing is generated requires a different vocabulary, something still being searched for. It will be as different in our time as talking and thinking about the solar system was in Copernicus's time.

The shift in thinking about cosmology in Copernicus's time also had long-term implications. A larger vision of Christian education will, too. Landing on the moon, satellites, information about Mars and other planets would not have been possible without re-mapping the heavens. The same will be true when children begin to absorb and activate the whole Christian language system at an early age. A re-blending of Copernicus's unity of art, religion, and science, which was displayed so wonderfully in his creativity five hundred years ago, may once again be part of the ministry of the local church.

Dava Sobel described in rich detail how Copernicus was engaged in the art, religion, and science of his time when he made his discovery.[18] He often wrote of the beauty of the heavens and translated poetry that interested him from Greek to Latin, integrating science and art. He was also a canon of the diocese, even though he was not permitted to say Mass, since he was not ordained. Still, he earned a doctor's degree in canon law in Italy while pursuing his cosmological studies there. His duties in the Cathedral Chapter were a brilliant blend of being a practicing physician and engaging in the business of the diocese—including a revision of currency as well as building a laboratory in which to study the stars. Blending science, religion, and art, as Copernicus did, can bring the church back to being on the frontier, the creative edge, of human endeavor.

Finally, like the new cosmology of Copernicus, a reorientation of the church around the mutual blessing of children and adults will take some getting used to. The pain, brilliance, and drama of the solar system's advocacy in the lives of Tycho Brahe

(1546–1601), Johannes Kepler (1571–1630), and Galileo Galilei (1564–1642) is well known. Those who advocate for the re-centering of the church around the mutual blessing of children and adults can also expect some difficulty—ambivalence, ambiguity, and indifference about children will likely be the response. Advocacy may be job-threatening but not life-threatening. What needs to be kept in mind, however, is that today there is no university in the world that still teaches the old pre-Copernican cosmology. Will something like that take place in a re-centered church?

Conclusion

A call to re-center the church around children is, indeed, crawling out on a limb, so we need to consider the tree from which the limb has grown to see how strong it might be. To do this we will explore the Montessori tradition from which Godly Play grew. The story of the first two generations of this tradition will be told in the next chapter.

2.

Foundations:

Montessori and the Montessorians

The story of the first two generations of Montessori religious education is an adventure story, as unlikely as that might seem. It involves founders and followers, pure and impure interpretations, strong women and men in early childhood education, two world wars, money, competing theories, an evolving method, and even sex resulting in a child born out of wedlock! Let's begin at the beginning with Maria Montessori herself.

The Founder of the Tradition: Maria Montessori (1870–1952)

Five major sources[1] will be used to tell Montessori's story, which is, as one of her biographers wrote, "much more complicated and interesting than the plaster saint her devoted followers have made her into."[2] Montessori was born in 1870, the year Italy became fully unified for the first time since the fall of the Roman Empire and she died in 1952, the year Dwight D. Eisenhower was elected president of the United States.

Montessori's Early Years

Montessori was born in the Adriatic seaport of Ancona, at a time when it was still the custom for women to carry water to their homes from the ancient fountain on the hill.[3] The family moved to Rome when Maria was five, and at twelve she surprised her parents by announcing that she wanted to be an engineer. She loved mathematics, so in the fall of 1883 she entered the *Regia Scuola Technica Michelangelo Buonarroti*.

As a girl, Maria probably participated in the customary rites of the Roman Catholic Church with other children her age, including her first communion in a pure, white dress. By the time she entered medical school, however, she "began her adult life as a freethinker."[4] It is clear that her idealism tended towards social reform and the rights of women, which sometimes put her at odds with the Roman Church of her day.

Montessori entered medical school in 1892 after taking some prerequisite courses. She was the only woman in her class and used a little rhyme to cope amiably with the frustrating comments and whistles in the hallways of this traditionally all-male preserve. "The harder you blow, the higher I go."[5] Fortunately she had allies on the faculty, such as Molischott, Celli, and Bonfigli. Like her, they were also interested in the social aspects of medicine, children, and the equality of women.[6] She graduated from the University of Rome in 1896 with distinction and was one of only a handful of young women in Italy to earn a degree in medicine since the unification.[7]

Centering and Re-Centering

After graduation Dr. Montessori went into private practice and worked in various clinics in Rome. She became known as *una donna nuova* (a new woman), so a few months after graduation she was selected to go to Berlin to speak at an international feminist congress. One day she spoke for socialist women without property and the next day her speech was for capitalist women who owned property. She was, as she said, the champion of all women, regardless of their circumstances.

Her public appearances charmed the antagonistic, male press, who wrote about how beautiful and well-spoken she was instead of what she had to say. Her style was, indeed, in contrast to the severe, masculine fashion for feminists of that day or the comfortable, baggy pants, called "bloomers," invented by Amelia Bloomer in the 1850s. If the press had actually listened to her they would have heard a sharply incisive but not strident mind at work.

Her 1896 addresses in Berlin announced that feminism had found "a crack in the ruins of Roman monuments and the heaps of Catholic prejudgments" to move forward despite all resistance.[8] She was equally critical of the *Congregazione di Carita* (The Congress of Charity) of the Roman Catholic Church and the Roman government's *Komitee Soccorso e Lavoro* (Relief and Work Committee).

In 1898 Dr. Giuseppe Montesano and Dr. Maria Montessori were appointed the co-directors of the Orthophrenic School for handicapped children. The two talented, young physicians had published papers together and in the same year as their appointment they founded a society in Rome called *Per la Donna* (For the Woman). Its goal was for men and women to collaborate in scientific and social fields.[9]

About this time she also noticed that the children she worked with sometimes fought for crumbs of bread, not to eat but to play with. They seemed to need stimulation rather than the enforced immobility that was the custom to provide for them. She also noticed they needed a sense of community, so she worked directly with the children to accomplish this and invited the less handicapped to help care for the rest.

To learn more about the children's need for stimulation she began to read the works of the French physicians Jean Itard (1775–1838) and his student Edouard Seguin (1812–1880). Following their lead, she began to systematically develop sensorial materials and have them manufactured.[10] She wrote that she had not seen such a complete a set of teaching materials anywhere. They were effective "in the hands of those who know how to apply them, . . . but unless rightly presented, they failed to attract the attention of the deficients."[11]

In the midst of this professional activity and creativity Dr. Montessori and Dr. Montesano grew close and had a son, Mario, who was born on March 31, 1898. His name was listed as Mario Pipilli, and Mancia Carlotta, the wet nurse who registered him, indicated that she would be responsible for nursing and raising the infant. The two families had agreed that the young doctors should not marry and that the incident would be kept private. In 1901 Dr. Montesano married, but Montessori never did.[12]

Montessori's interest in her work at the clinic and an academic career in psychiatry waned. She left the school in 1901, the same year that Montesano married, and returned to graduate school to study psychology and education. She began to lecture about these subjects in Rome while continuing to speak at national and international conferences. The subject of her speeches, however, shifted from women's rights to the education of children as part of a social movement on behalf of *the new woman*. It was also during this time that she began a custom, carried on for several years, of retiring for two weeks each summer at a convent near Bologna to meditate among the nuns.[13]

Maria Montessori's life gradually found a new center in children's education. She wrote, "Our educational aim with very young children must be to *aid the spontaneous development of the mental, spiritual, and physical personality*, and not to make of the child a cultured individual in the commonly accepted sense of the term."[14] She stood firmly against the artificial imposition of cultural information by rote and authoritarian methods, because this approach did not serve the child's real nature. She urged teachers "to guard that spiritual fire," which expresses the child's "real nature unspoiled" in order "to set it free from the oppressive and degrading yoke of society."[15]

During these early days, Montessori engaged the whole child by her warmth, energy, sense of humor, and curiosity and always urged teachers to "follow the child" to discover what to do as a teacher. Once in Rome, during a teacher training, she tied the young women to the pillars in the classroom so they had to observe, as she said, like one might watch the planets moving about the sun. This prevented them from intervening too soon at signs of disturbance. They had to consider where the intervention might best be made to restore the self-regulating order indirectly from *within* the group instead of imposing it directly on the children from the outside. Today one can still see some Montessori teachers, including myself, go sit down and watch calmly for a moment before guiding the children toward self-regulating order. This allows one's vision to clear, inner agitation to subside, and adult projections to be swept aside to see what will be best for the children's long-term growth.

Montessori considered her classrooms to be laboratories for experimenting with her method and the sensorial materials she had created, but above all she wanted to discover the child's true nature. She was interested in "education for life," so she needed to know what kind of life children actually had.

Montessori respected children and was curious about their true nature, so she began to experiment with the environment to see if she could make it more appropriate for them. This is why she began to use little tables and chairs, which were very radical for her time. She also allowed the children to move around and choose their own work from among constructive alternatives. These changes from traditional education allowed the children to relax and use their energy for learning rather than wasting it on trying to adapt to an environment designed to meet the needs of adults. This also allowed their true nature to be revealed. What Montessori saw in this open setting astonished her and drew people to her schools to watch the children, as if children had never been truly seen before.

The children in the Montessori environment showed how much they loved learning and that they enjoyed order. They remained absorbed for long periods of time on projects of their own choosing, demonstrating a long attention span previously unnoticed. Montessori began to call the child she saw appearing the "normal child," because what we usually see is abnormal. This is because children in customary classrooms are under stress, as they try to adjust to environments set up for the convenience of the adults. The normal children loved silence and enjoyed assuming responsibility for taking care of their own classroom. They cooperated to prepare and share meals together and work in the garden. They were concerned about and worked together to decide what was fair for their classroom community. Above all, they revealed that they were deeply spiritual.[16]

Montessori Education and Religion

Christian educators are usually not aware of Montessori's deep interest in religion and many Montessorians have forgotten or never noticed this. For example, she selected Epiphany, January 6, 1907, to open her first *Casa dei Bambini* (Children's House). She read from Isaiah 60:1–5 and concluded her remarks by saying, "This Children's House can become a new Jerusalem."[17] At that moment, however, all she had to begin with were her fifty children from the surrounding tenement houses, some sparsely furnished rooms, her experience with the handicapped children, and a grand vision.

Mario Montessori discussed these early days in 1961 at a London conference concerning "The Spiritual Hunger of the Modern Child." He responded to the question about whether Maria had trained the children to display the characteristics she called normal or, as she said, had merely removed the obstacles that prevented them from being themselves. Mario stressed that she did not believe at first what she was seeing and then, "this positivist, who disbelieved in religion" had to admit that what she was seeing was true. He then read from *The Secret of Childhood* to quote her as saying, "I stood respectfully before the children, saying to myself: 'Who are you then? Have I perhaps met with the children who were held in Christ's arms and to whom divine words were spoken? I will follow you to enter with you into the Kingdom of Heaven.'" She did not "convert" them, he said, but they converted her.[18] This means that when Montessori urged teachers to "follow the child," she was really urging them to be more than keen observers. She was also encouraging them to follow the child *as their vocation and spiritual practice.*

To deny the child's "religious sentiment," Montessori wrote, is "to commit a pedagogical error similar to that of denying,

a priori, to the child, the love of learning for learning's sake."[19]
She thought that when religion is not included in the education of young children two distortions occur, the loss of equi-
librium in the moral life and religious fanaticism. Fanaticism
is the result of "a life deprived of spirituality." Usually the rem-
edy comes too late and is applied too artificially for the child's
full development.[20]

Montessori wanted Raphael's *Madonna della Seggiola*
(Madonna of the Chair) to be hung in a prominent place in her
schools.[21] This was to remind *both* the children and the adults
of their spirituality and the importance of their relationship
with each other. Sometimes you will still see this painting hanging in Montessori schools, but seldom will you see it hanging at
the child's eye level so children as well as adults can reflect on
its meaning.

Maria Montessori called her teachers "directresses,"
because she considered teaching to be guiding children's learning rather than imposing it.[22] This is why the spiritual nature
of the teacher was so important. She wrote in *The Montessori
Method* that the ideal teacher has a soul that combines "the
self-sacrificing spirit of the scientist with the reverent love of
the disciple of Christ."[23]

In 1910, the same year she resigned her academic position and had her name removed from the list of practicing
physicians in Rome, Maria Montessori and her closest followers swore before the Blessed Sacrament to remain committed
to the Roman Catholic Church and to dedicate their lives to
serving children.

Her views of religion no doubt became more complex as she
became a citizen of the world during the next forty years, but
two years before her death she was still discussing the founding
of a religious order to work with children, along the lines of the

lay Dominican, Franciscan, and Carmelite Third Orders.[24] Her last "public utterance" was written for the Catholic Montessori Guild in England, but she died before she could present it.[25]

Sometimes the influence of the Mass on the Montessori method is not fully appreciated, although Montessori discussed how the Mass is "the pedagogical method" of the Roman Catholic Church.[26] This connection was impossible for me to miss, however, especially during the decade I was the canon educator at Christ Church Cathedral in downtown Houston.

During Holy Communion the elements were placed on the corporal, which is a linen cloth smoothed out on the altar like a Montessori underlay. The chalice (a cup for the wine) and the paten (a plate for the bread) as well as the ciborium (for extra bread) and cruets for water and wine, were carefully placed on the corporal. These beautiful objects were handled with a dignity that respects their deep meaning. All this resonates with the careful laying out of a Montessori lesson.

When everything is set, the narrative moves by little steps from the past, to the present celebration, and into the future as the congregation leaves the church after receiving Holy Communion. Montessori often took something from human history, such as the discovery of the Pythagorean theorem, and turned it into a teaching material to be presented with dignity and care so the children could discover its deepest meaning. Just as in the Mass, when "the material" was put away the children could move forward with their lives enriched.

Thea and I taught the ten-to-twelve-year-old Godly Play class at the cathedral for ten years during the education hour, so I was either coming from being the celebrant at the eight o'clock or the nine o'clock Eucharist to sit on the floor with the children, or I was on my way to be the celebrant at the eleven o'clock liturgy. This interplay between Godly Play and

Holy Communion took place at least five hundred times during those ten years. Sometimes with a smile, I let the interplay blend together.

Maria Montessori's mother, who had been against any mention of her daughter's child, died in December of 1912 at the age of seventy-two. The next year young Mario came to live with Dr. Montessori and her father in the apartment on Via Principessa Clotilde, near the Piazza del Popolo in Rome, looking out over the vast Pincio gardens. This became a meeting place for the talented young women who were her early followers and where she held her early courses.[27] In the midst of all this activity, however, she never lost sight of the spiritual life of teachers and the children she worked with. An opportunity to develop this continuing interest appeared in 1916.

The Religious Education Experiment in Barcelona: 1916–1936

In 1915 Anna Maccheroni, one of Montessori's earliest and most devoted followers, prepared the way for Montessori to come to Barcelona. Maccheroni set up a small class in the city and contacted the Benedictine Abbot of the Shrine of Montserrat. He invited her to participate in a liturgical congress held at the abbey about an hour away, which had been a place of pilgrimage for over a thousand years.

Maccheroni proposed to the conference that teaching the liturgy to young children, three to six years of age, was quite possible. Pius X (1835–1914) was the scourge of modernism but he was also a pastoral pope who issued a decree just before his death about the communion of children. He declared that they should be admitted to Holy Communion earlier than the previous custom and he called for a more adequate preparation for children to participate in worship. These two events combined to bring approval and cooperation from the Catholic Church for the Barcelona experiment.

The work began in earnest when Dr. Montessori arrived in Barcelona in 1916 from California and after a visit to Rome, where her father had died. In California she had spoken at the Panama-Pacific International Exposition in San Francisco, where a demonstration classroom had been set up with glass walls for several months in 1915. She had also conducted at least one training course of several months during this visit to the West Coast. After arrival in Barcelona, Montessori secured funding for her institute for two years from the Catalonian government and settled there. Barcelona was her home until 1936.

Mario had married Helen Christie in 1917 in California when he was about nineteen. His mother's last visit to the United States was a quiet, personal visit in 1918. It was also in that year that Mario and his bride moved to Barcelona to join his mother and the work of the movement. They had four children—Marlina, Mario Jr., Renilde, and Rolando— but subsequently divorced. Mario's first wife returned to the United States.

As an aside, one can't help wondering what it would have been like for Mario's young bride to have had Dr. Maria Montessori as her mother-in-law, living in Spain, far from California! In 1914 Montessori had been quoted in *Life* magazine as saying "We believe in taking the baby away from his or her mother just as soon as the child is born. That is because (t)he mother does not know how to care for her offspring. Parents require much training before they are to be trusted."[28]

Rita Kramer has provided a vivid picture of Montessori's model school and training center in Barcelona. "The institute was housed in an old building of traditional Spanish architecture with spacious grounds, gardens, orchards, and winding, palm-lined paths. There were little pools with fountains and goldfish, sheds and cages for pets, all under the brilliant southern sky."[29] Montessori had always tried to blend nature, art, order and learning.

At the center of the school was the most beautiful of all the school's interior spaces. Local artists had furnished the white and gold chapel with statues, paintings, and furniture reduced in size to make the environment as accessible as possible to the children. The 1929 edition of Standing's *The Child in the Church* includes a large picture of the elaborate altar with its beautiful carvings.

A young priest, Mossen Iginio Angles, was chosen to oversee the children's worship and religious education, mostly conceived of as regular involvement in worship and preparation for their first communion. To prepare for their first communion the children grew the wheat in the meadow to make the bread for their first communion host. They processed through the school with their bunches of wheat tied with colorful ribbons when it was ripe. They then ground the wheat into flour to prepare the dough, which was stamped with each child's chosen symbol, and baked into bread. The wine was made from grapes, also grown at the school and harvested by the children. The unity of life and liturgy was built into the school's natural routine.[30]

During this time Montessori wrote several booklets about religious education.[31] In *Children Living in the Church* she observed that the establishment of the Barcelona experiment meant that ". . . the Montessori Method was furnished with a long-sought opportunity of penetrating deeper into the life of the child's soul, and of thus fulfilling its true educational mission."[32]

At Montessori's death the memoir of a Barcelona teacher was published, which told how in 1916, at the beginning of the Barcelona experiment, Montessori had been heard sobbing at Mass on Christmas Eve at Our Lady of Pompei. This made her one with the Catalonians, because, as they said, she had cried with them. Montessori later told Maccheroni:

> I seek to discover the man in the child, to see in him the true human spirit, the design of the Creator: the scientific and religious truth. It is to this end that I apply my method of study, which respects human nature. I don't need to teach anything to children: it is they who, placed in a favorable environment, teach me, reveal to me spiritual secrets as long as their souls have not been deformed.[33]

When the Spanish Civil War broke out in 1936, Dr. Montessori and her family escaped from Barcelona on an English warship. They traveled immediately to the already-scheduled Oxford Montessori Congress, but they had no home to return to after the Congress was over. Ada Pierson, a young Dutch woman at the congress, understood this. She and her family, the Pierson banking family, arranged for Montessori and her family to move to Holland. Mario and Ada soon married and Holland became the Montessori home and the center of the movement. The headquarters was established in Amsterdam, where it remains.

Montessori and Mario traveled to India in 1939 to give a three-month course and conduct a lecture tour. India, as a colony of Britain, declared war on Nazi Germany the same year. The Rome-Berlin Axis had been formed in 1936. Since Maria and Mario carried Italian passports, they were "the enemy." Mario was interned but freed on his mother's seventieth birthday and they continued to train Montessori teachers during World War II. Meanwhile Ada and her family cared for Mario's four children during the Nazi occupation of Holland. Mario and Maria Montessori returned to Holland after the War, but in 1947, the same year India was granted independence, they returned so Montessori could give a course with special attention to infants and early childhood.

Her last course in India described how young children absorb the environment unconsciously through a psycho-chemical process, which first incorporates the structures needed for creativity and then the creative life begins. In language, for example, the structure of one's native language is absorbed physically as well as intellectually so the words shape how they are spoken correctly. The words are then inserted into slots in assimiliated patterns to make meaning. These lectures were the basis for Montessori's book *The Absorbent Mind*.[34]

Toward the end of *The Absorbent Mind*, Montessori tried to sum up the spiritual complexity she had experienced in her long life and relate it to the energy she had first sensed in children when she was a young physician. "I would like to say a word about this reality, and also about the sayings of the poets and the prophets. This force that we call love is the greatest energy of the universe. But I am using an inadequate expression, for it is more than an energy: it is creation itself. I should put it better if I were to say: 'God is love.' "[35]

After she returned to Amsterdam she continued to travel some, but she was eighty now and travel was difficult. She returned to Rome for the last time in 1951 and returned to Amsterdam. The next year she and Mario went to the North Sea shore for a rest. She was seated in the garden of friends in Noordwijk aan Zee when she died. Since she had asked to be buried where she fell, as a testimony to the universality of her work, her grave may be found today in the small cemetery of the Roman Catholic Church in Noordwijk aan Zee.[36]

The Discovery of the Child, published just before her death, was the last revision of her *Montessori Method,* first published in English some forty years before. Only a few traces of the earlier, explicitly Christian themes remained. Instead of mentioning the "disciples of Christ" when describing the teacher she wrote, "But let us strive to pour into a single soul the keen spirit of sacrifice of a scientist and the ineffable ecstasy of such a mystic, and we shall then have the perfect spirit of our 'teacher.' "[37] Both expressions, early and late, demonstrated the two sides to Montessori's own personality: the careful, objective observer and the open, relational mystic.

The Discovery of the Child also included a section called "Religious Education." Montessori briefly described her work in Barcelona and noted that the sensitive period for religion was before the age of six years. She then concluded: "The experiment in religious education was eventually abolished in our Children's Houses because it was aimed exclusively at instruction in Catholicism, which lends itself to exercises in moving about and preparing various objects, whereas there is no place for such activities in religions that are almost entirely abstract."[38] Would Montessori's experiments in religious education survive? The answer to this question depended on her followers.

The Movement and Montessori Religious Education

When Montessori made her foundational discoveries about children's spirituality and education most everything was under her control. The *Casa dei Bambini* in the San Lorenzo District of Rome was like her private laboratory. Her aides were devoted to her and to the project. They were like extensions of her personal creativity and energy. As they worked together with the children, life was stimulating, challenging, and emotionally satisfying. It was in this setting that she discovered the "normal" spirituality of children.

The change from pursuing an idea to leading a movement and then to heading a multi-national organization is a story in itself, but our concern here is to see whether Montessori religious education will survive these many organizational changes and the relational dynamics of founders and followers. This part of the story is about the rich variety of followers, shown by representative types, and the right combination of qualities to carry this work forward. It is also about how every generation must make such transitions, so in terms of Montessori religious education these generational transitions can be expected to continue.

One of Montessori's early followers was Anna Maccheroni (1876–1965).[39] She was often referred to as "dear old Maccheroni" although she was six years younger than Montessori. Montessori trusted her for good reason. She was loyal and got things done. Maccheroni set up Montessori schools in Rome, Milan, Barcelona, England, Scotland and probably elsewhere. She helped create the early Montessori music program and was the one who began to chart children's concentration during the school day, which became an important part of Montessori theory. She was even Montessori's first biographer. Maccheroni seemed like the perfect follower, so one wonders why she did not carry on with the religious education experiments. She had been very active with the project in Barcelona.

Perhaps there was something about her relationship with Montessori that made it increasingly difficult for Montessori to think of Maccheroni as a collaborator as they grew older.

Montessori longed for colleagues with more independence, but when she worked with independent-minded followers she found them hard to trust. This placed her followers in a double bind concerning their independence as colleagues and was an ironic paradox for the founder of an approach to education that stressed self-direction for children!

Phyllis Wallbank, who founded the Gatehouse School in London in 1948, remembered talking with Montessori about Maccheroni:

> Oh, dear old Signorina Macaroni. Montessori said to me (laugh)—well Macaroni adored Montessori and Montessori found Macaroni a horrible hindrance and nuisance because she was sort of passionate about her and was a nuisance in that way. Montessori said to me it wouldn't be heaven if Macaroni was there! (laughter) Well, if someone is passionate it can be an awful nuisance.[40]

There is, no doubt, an element of truth in this, especially as Maccheroni grew older and more eccentric. For example, she was in England when World War II broke out and had to be moved by friends out of London to keep her from being interned, because she was so outspoken against the English.[41] She was then moved to Scotland, where anti-English sentiments were more acceptable, which explains the improbability that her biography of Montessori was first published in English and in Scotland instead of in Italian by an Italian publisher.

Maccheroni had been one of the early followers who gathered around Maria Montessori like nuns around their mother superior. There were happy jokes about this and many followers seemed quite comfortable adopting a life style that approximated the religious vows of poverty, obedience, and celibacy (or at least foregoing marriage). Fortunately, some of the young women around Montessori were also independently wealthy. Adelia Pyle and Helen Parkhurst had to write to their families to forward them money to pay the expenses of the Montessori entourage while living in California.[42] Anna Maccheroni, like many of the early followers, may have been too involved with Montessori the person, rather than the whole vision of Montessori education, to carry the concept of religious education forward.

If her devoted followers could not carry on, perhaps, it would be Montessori's son. Mario Montessori took over leadership of the Association Montessori Internationale (AMI) when his mother died in 1952. He developed an organization that included national societies, training centers on four continents, and continuing activities such as congresses, publications, and research. He was also one of the few males in the movement. Others included Claude Claremont, Albert Joosten, and E. M. Standing.[43]

Mario Montessori trained a nucleus of assistants, who together with the surviving pupils of Dr. Montessori became the teacher-trainers to continue the movement. He was dedicated to preserving the purity of the precious inheritance his mother left him. For example in 1952 Nancy Rambusch went to Paris from the United States to attend the Tenth Annual International Montessori Congress sponsored by the French government. She had hoped to meet Maria Montessori there, but she had already died in May of that year. As Nancy Rambusch told the story to Phyllis Povell, she met with Mario, as the new head of the organization, and shared with him her dream about setting up a "Montessori type" school. She probably thought that he would be pleased since Montessori education had nearly died out in the United States after a great burst of enthusiasm from 1911–1917. He responded, "Madame, there is no such thing as a 'Montessori type' school, there is only a 'Montessori school.' "[44]

Nancy Rambusch set up her school near Greenwich, Connecticut anyway. The Whitby School held its first classes in 1958 in an old barn. In 1960 she went on to found the American Montessori Society (AMS), which headquartered there, but later moved its offices to New York City, where they are now.

Mario had begun to manage the business and travel details for his mother when he and his family moved to Barcelona. As his mother grew older, he remained her companion and sounding board, but realized that the organization could no longer be tied so closely to Roman Catholicism, nor any particular religion. It was now a world-wide educational movement encompassing many cultures and religions. He had neither the interest nor the opportunity to carry on the experiments in religious education during the next thirty years. He died in 1982.

Perhaps Phyllis Wallbank would be the one to carry this tradition forward. She had the talent, energy, and interest to do this and she was married to the Reverend Dr. Newell Wallbank, rector of St. Bartholomew the Great in London. Her interest in religion was serious. She had quietly became a Roman Catholic after becoming involved with Montessori, even though her husband was an Anglican priest.

She had happily helped Montessori at no cost when Montessori called on her to organize trainings, help with workshops, or examine teachers for her in Europe or England. She even organized the last International Montessori Congress in London to involve Maria Montessori herself, shortly before Montessori's death.

Wallbank, however, allowed non-Montessorians to observe in her school. When Montessori found out about this she cut off all communication with her and removed her school from the official AMI list. Nevertheless, Wallbank remained devoted to the Montessori method and helped the movement in ways she could while being a *persona non grata*.

Wallbank had founded her Montessori school in the Gatehouse of St. Bartholomew the Great in 1948 and led its growth until she retired in 1979. The Gatehouse School still thrives in London and the Phyllis Wallbank Educational Trust provides educational scholarships for graduates to attend university. Despite her many contributions to Montessori education she could not be the bridge to the future for Montessori religious education, even if she would have liked to have been.

Helen Parkhurst was, perhaps, the most talented educator of Montessori's followers in the United States. Montessori respected and trusted her so much that she convinced her to be the demonstration teacher in the glass-walled classroom at the Panama-Pacific Exposition in San Francisco in 1915. She had hoped that Parkhurst would lead the movement in the United States, but Parkhurst had other ideas. She set up the Dalton Plan, named after a high school she developed in Dalton, Massachusetts, and in 1919 established The Dalton School in New York City, which still flourishes today.

Parkhurst only mentioned Montessori in passing in her 1922 book called *Education on the Dalton Plan*. She did, however, quote Edward Seguin at the head of her book about discoveries coming "simultaneously from so many quarters that the title of a single individual to discovery is always contested and seems clearly to belong to God manifested through man." There was clearly a religious dimension to her, but she was more passionate about education than religion, so neither was she the one to carry Montessori religious education forward.

There were also people who were more passionate about religion than education. Adelia Pyle is a good example. She had moved to Spain from America with Montessori, but disappeared from the movement about 1924. She had been one of the first to train in Rome with Montessori from outside Italy and Montessori relied on her gift for languages to translate for her for about a decade. She was so trusted that she was selected to be the translator for Montessori at the Panama-Pacific International Exposition and seemed to fill a daughter's role in Montessori's inner circle.

Adelia Pyle converted to Roman Catholicism while in Spain with Montessori, taking the name of Mary, which resulted in her being disinherited from her wealthy Presbyterian family. After her time with Montessori in Spain she moved on to Rome and then to San Giovanni Rotondo in southeastern Italy. She went there to seek the spiritual guidance of Padre Pio, who was famous for his visions, stigmata, and many good works, such as building a huge hospital and research center in San Giovanni Rotondo. Mary lived the last forty-five years of her life in close association with Padre Pio. She and her mother reconciled and she bought a large house near the monastery, which she maintained as a guesthouse.[45]

The right combination of religious interest, educational talent, the confidence and skill to express Montessori's ideas, and the ability to remain connected with Maria Montessori was hard to find, but one person appeared who had all of these characteristics. This was E. M. Standing. He was the primary person who helped build the bridge for the second generation to pass over to the third generation of Montessori religious education.

The Transition To a New Generation:
E. M. Standing

Ted Standing was born on September 18,1887, in Tananarive, Madagascar, to a family of Quaker missionaries. When he was about six years old his family sent him back to England for his schooling, as a boarding student with fellow Quakers. He then went to the University of Leeds, a mostly red-brick campus located in the north of England. He graduated from Leeds with a B.S. in biology in 1909 and the following year earned a Diploma in Education at Cambridge University. He then went to Germany for a brief period to study at the University of Freiburg and disappeared from history for about a decade from 1910 to 1921, probably teaching in various schools in England.

Standing met Montessori in 1921 at a time when the national and international Montessori groups in England were struggling to define their roles. This became so intense that *Punch*, an influential English magazine of humor and satire, could not restrain comment:

> Sing, Muse, the tragic story of the Montessorian split
> And the lurid possibilities arising out of it,
> Revealing how "paedologists," though normally urbane
> May develop, on occasion, quite a first-class fighting strain.[46]

This controversy continued in England and also appeared in the United States after World War II, but Standing was not distracted or disillusioned, because of his broad and solid foundation as an educator. Above all, he had found the method and person he was looking for to guide his spiritual and educational quest.

Standing attended his first training course in London. During the course, Montessori arranged for him to go to India for a year as the tutor to the many children of the Sarabhai family. When he returned to Europe he took the course again in London or, perhaps, in Barcelona. His notes from these two courses may be found in the E. M. Standing Center at Seattle University. From then on he made himself useful in the movement.

Two photographs found among Standing's effects after he died may shed some light on his character.[47] One shows him standing in a slightly rumpled suit in the *Piazza San Marco* among the pigeons in Venice with a bird on his head. The other photograph shows him, again formally attired in a suit, lounging in a tree. Standing was like an itinerant lay friar with little interest in anything but the education and religious life of children, which was part of his own religious quest. He wrote that Montessori, "never treated educational problems on a purely technical or utilitarian level. Her appeal was always to the spirit"[48] and Standing responded in kind. Like Adelia Pyle, Phyllis Wallbank, and a few other Montessorians he converted to Roman Catholicism.[49] He happily traveled where and when needed—Barcelona, Rome, London, and elsewhere—working "in collaboration with the Dottoressa."

One of the tasks Standing set for himself in the movement was to help communicate Montessori's ideas to a larger audience. In 1929 he published a collection of her articles, translated into English, as *The Child in the Church*. His interest in the religious life of children could also be seen in his correspondence with people all over the world and as a founding member of the Catholic Montessori Guild in England.

Standing loved Dante and was legendary in Montessori circles for quoting Shakespeare. In addition to his Montessori writing he wrote poetry, short stories, and articles about education such as "Montessori Practice and Thomistic Principles" and "The Narrative Method Versus the Catechism." His more literary writings appeared in the *Atlantic*, *Sower*, *Irish Rosary*, *America*, and *The Times* (London). Mostly, however, his main purpose as a writer was to try to better communicate Montessori's "fundamental principles."

Standing published three books the last decade of his life: *Maria Montessori: Her Life and Work*, *The Montessori Revolution*, and a greatly expanded *The Child in the Church*. In the archives of the E. M. Standing Center at Seattle University are his manuscripts, which show how he worked. He cut out corrections typed on pieces of paper and pasted them over his typed draft, much like we do today electronically.

Standing's *Maria Montessori: Her Life and Work* is still in print and is his most widely read publication, but it included little about Montessori's interest in religious education, "striking and original as it is,"[50] as he noted. He considered Montessori's experiments about teaching religion beyond the scope of this book, but it was permeated with Christian assumptions and language. He wrote that "sin blurs our vision of the child" and the "two sins" of pride and anger especially need to be overcome by the "directress," who should exemplify "the self-sacrificing spirit of the scientist with the love of the disciple of Christ."[51] As the book took shape, Montessori read the manuscript and commented on matters of historical detail, but she died before it was published on the fiftieth anniversary of the opening of her first school.

Fr. William Codd, S.J., professor of education and psychology at Seattle University, was part of the Roman Catholic network of Montessorians and had set up a Montessori training program at the university. He invited Standing to come teach there, but Standing was seventy-five years old, living in Ireland, and was not in good health. Despite all, he moved to Seattle, still making himself useful in the Montessori movement.

Standing's *The Montessori Revolution in Education* was published in 1962 in the United States just after he arrived. He had been working on it for a long time and distilled this book about Montessori into concise, striking vignettes with photographs of children to illustrate Montessori's principles. This was the book, more than the other two, that showed his down-to-earth idealism about education and religion at its best.

First of all, he called it "tragic" when people do not engage children's spirituality during the sensitive period for religion, which Montessori had said was before six years of age. This was like, he added wryly, saying that children should put off deciding what their favorite dish is until they are all grown up. Furthermore, to avoid any undue prejudice about this selection, they should not be given any food until they are adults![52]

He also asked us to consider how to help children integrate their body-mind-spirit unity. His answer was in a vignette about a child polishing a brass model of a chalice and paten. The first level is physical. The child is merely polishing. At the next level the child realizes how this polishing preserves the beauty of the cup and plate and how this act helps care for the environment of the classroom. The third level is engaged when the child consciously ponders the meaning of God's presence in Holy Communion while polishing.

He was concerned that many children did not have an opportunity to develop their spirituality. When the child's environment does not include teaching materials for religion, it is impossible to realize how important religion is to the child.

This is like building an environment for monkeys with nothing to climb on. Without anything to climb on it is impossible to see that monkeys are naturally developed for climbing.

Standing was also sensitive to the rhythm of the child's life and compared it to the eternal present of the mystic. Adults need to become like children to appreciate "their majestic inner rhythm, which is more of eternity than of time."[53] At the end of *The Montessori Revolution* he wrote, following Montessori, "The child and the adult are two distinct parts of humanity, which must work together and interpenetrate in harmony with reciprocal aid. They are not merely a succession of phases in the individual's life."[54]

At the end of *The Montessori Revolution* Standing revisited a recurring controversy he had already lived through more than once in other countries. Such battles only distracted from finding what is best for children. In his newly adopted country the combatants were the Association Montessori Internationale (AMI), founded in 1929, and the American Montessori Society (AMS), founded in 1960 by Nancy McCormick Rambush. He advocated for both groups in a respectful, factual, and indirect way as this book concluded to keep the focus on children.

The main bridge-building between the generations that Standing did for Montessori religious education was his greatly expanded version of *The Child in the Church*. The transition can be seen in the book's structure. Montessori's original chapters remained from the 1929 edition, but in the 1965 version he added three chapters of his own with one chapter each by other transition figures: Mother Isabel Eugenie, Marchesa Sofia Cavalletti, and Monsieur and Madame Lanternier. He concluded the book with three more chapters he wrote that described tentative lesson plans and teaching materials.

When this book appeared in 1965, Sofia Cavalletti and Gianna Gobbi's first book, *Teaching Doctrine and Liturgy*, had just been translated into English in 1964 and Vatican II, which addressed the relationship between the Roman Catholic Church and the modern world, was drawing to a close.

In *The Child in the Church* Standing thanked the Sisters of Providence in Seattle for "their genial and generous hospitality, which has enabled me to devote my energies entirely to Montessori work in a 'Home' which has become a real home to me."[55] This was poignant, because Standing had never really had a home since he left Madagascar as a boy. Phyllis Wallbank, a long time friend of Standing's, remembered that he "merely went and stayed with people for months on end and then went to another person and stayed there."[56]

In *The Child in the Church* Standing let the reader know he was full of plans, despite being almost eighty years old, for a new book about children and religion, which he said was half finished. He was also advocating for a new international version of a Catholic Montessori Guild. When he died, March 4, 1967, letters of sadness came to Seattle University from all over the world. Mario Montessori wrote from the Netherlands. Friends from India wrote. There were many others.

Standing left his estate, including royalties from the sale of his books, to Seattle University to support Montessori education. Fr. Codd established the E. M. Standing Center in his honor. Today the center is directed by Dr. John Chattin-McNichols, professor of education at the university. His Montessori training was from the AMI course in Bergamo, Italy, and he later became the president of the American Montessori Society. Standing would have loved having his Montessori heir trained by and active in both AMI and AMS, focusing on the best that both have to offer the child.

Conclusion

This brings to an end the story of the first two generations of Montessorians, who laid the foundation for Montessori religious education. In the next chapter we will tell the story of the third generation by concentrating on the work of Sofia Cavalletti and Gianna Gobbi. They not only consolidated what had taken place before them but brilliantly extended it. We will also meet Godly Play, which grew out of the first three generations of this tradition.

3.

Transitions:

Montessorians and Godly Play

When Maria Montessori died in 1952 and E. M. Standing died in 1967 the story of Montessori religious education did not end. This chapter is about the third and fourth generations of this tradition. Sofia Cavalletti will represent the third generation and I will represent the fourth. We both specialized in Christian education, so the narrative narrows specifically to that theme, as we move on toward the future.

Now that we have come this far, it is time to ask if the story we are telling actually qualifies as a "tradition" of spirituality. Philip Sheldrake's life-long study of Christian spirituality has moved away from an exclusive emphasis on the "spiritual, cultural and social elites" to include a broader spectrum of people's practices, but he has never discussed traditions of *children's* spiritual guidance. Children's spirituality is important in itself, but it also influences adult spirituality, both by means of the children we once were and by the children around us. Is this history we have been recounting "a passing phase" or is there "a great deal more than the practice of a single exercise of piety or devotion" at work?[1]

Sheldrake developed three criteria to establish a tradition. First, the spiritual practice needs to have moved beyond a single individual and group of followers. There needs to be "a generation of practitioners that had no first-hand experience of the founder(s) or origins of the tradition." In this chapter our story moves well beyond people who knew Maria Montessori firsthand. Second, "certain classic texts or documentation or structures for the transmission of the tradition" need to have been established. Each of the four generations of Montessori religious education has produced such texts. Third, the "spiritual wisdom" needs to have "shown itself clearly capable of moving beyond its own time and place of origin." Montessori's first interest in children's spirituality is now over a century old and two of its key expressions today, the Catechesis of the Good Shepherd and Godly Play, are used all over the world and are still expanding. It is with some confidence, then, that we can speak of the Montessori approach to children's spiritual guidance as a *tradition*.

This chapter will be simple in outline, despite being complex in other ways. The story of Cavalletti's life and the influences on her work will be outlined and then the same will be done for me. The third section will discuss the interplay between Catechesis of the Good Shepherd, developed by Cavalletti and Gianna Gobbi, and Godly Play, developed by Jerome and Thea Berryman.

Sofia Cavalletti (1917–2011)

Sofia Cavalletti was clearly the leading figure in the third generation of Montessori religious educators, but the more one learns about Cavalletti, the more one realizes the importance of Gianna Gobbi (1920–2002) as her collaborator. Gobbi contributed her Montessori training and experience with young children to Cavalletti's knowledge of the Bible, theology, and her astonishing gift for languages. My primary relationship, however, was with Cavalletti.

Sofia Cavalletti was born in Rome on August 21, 1917, in the room where she later had her study. She was the daughter of Giorgio and Giulia Cavalletti. Her father was a magistrate in Rome. The city was much smaller in 1917 than it is today and was still dominated by the aristocracy. Sofia's family was one of the important families, moving about the city with a kind of confidence and privilege that has mostly disappeared or is, at least, harder to see today by the occasional visitor like myself.[2]

In 1870, when Maria Montessori was born, Rome had 220,000 inhabitants. When Sofia was four years old there were 692,000 people. In 1935 the population reached one million for the first time since 50 BCE. Today the city has 2,700,000 people.

The Cavalletti apartments, near the Piazza Navona, had been in her family on her mother's side for about three hundred years. Eugenio Pacelli was born in the same apartment building, called the Palazzo Pediconi, in 1876, but the family moved nearby in 1880. Pacelli was elected Pope Pius XII on his birthday in March of 1939 at the briefest conclave in the Roman Church's history: one day and three ballots. Sofia was about twelve at the time.

Sofia Cavalletti was a baby when World War I began and a young woman during World War II. She was first educated at home, as was customary for little girls of her station in life. Her mother taught her to read, a moment that she remembered

vividly. She gave her mother "all her money" out of gratitude. It was three coins, not even adding up to the sum of one
lira. Sofia found these coins among her mother's effects after
she died.

Sofia was five years old in 1922, when Mussolini became
prime minister. At age ten, she left home to attend school and
discovered that she had a great capacity for languages, learning
Latin and Greek with great ease. She continued for five years
and then should have gone on to the *liceo* for three more years
before university, but for some reason, perhaps the unsettled
political events in Rome, this did not happen, which frustrated
her. Between the world wars Sofia's days were taken up by
school, riding horses "on the other side of the river," going to
the Cavalletti villa, and the other pleasures of an old world that
would soon vanish.

One day when I asked Sofia about living in Rome during
World War II, she told me that she could still hear the boots of
the German troops, marching in the streets. Mussolini was
arrested in 1943 by the king, who was negotiating a peace
treaty with the advancing Allied troops. The Germans res-
cued Mussolini and took over Rome for 270 terrible days.
On June 5, 1943, Rome was liberated by the allied armies
and in 1946 Sofia passed her exams to enter the University of Rome. The official name for the University of Rome
is *La Sapienza—Università di Roma*, but it is often called
simply called *La Sapienze* (Wisdom). It was founded in
1303 and was where Maria Montessori graduated from
medical school.

Two people influenced Cavalletti's professional life more
than any others. One was Eugenio Zolli, the former chief rabbi
of Rome, who influenced her life as a biblical scholar. The other
major influence was Maria Montessori. Cavalletti met Zolli in

1946 and the influence of Montessori's work began in 1954, two years after Montessori's death.

The Influence of Zolli

Zolli's autobiography, *Before the Dawn*, was first published in English in 1954. In his author's note, Zolli expressed his appreciation for "my valued assistant at the university, Sofia Cavalletti, who typed and revised the first draft, offering very useful criticisms."[3] In the book he told the story of his life and dramatic baptism as a Roman Catholic, as the Germans were being driven out of Rome.[4]

Zolli lived the rest of his life quietly at the *Gregorianum* (the Pontifical Gregorian University) in Rome, founded in 1551 by St. Ignatius of Loyola. Zolli went to Mass there every morning and stayed afterwards to pray. He taught Hebrew studies and biblical exegesis at the Pontifical Biblical Institute as well as at other places in the city including the University of Rome, where he met Sofia Cavalletti.

Sofia remembered that she was especially struck by the connections he drew between the prophets and the beatitudes of Jesus. He also showed how Christianity completed Judaism, which would influence her curriculum for the Catechesis of the Good Shepherd. She was very active in Jewish and Roman Catholic relations and was always very animated when she told me about her latest trip to Jerusalem. Mostly, however, it was Zolli's "purity of heart" that left a lasting impression on her. She would later find such purity of heart for herself through her work with children.

Sofia Cavalletti was one of the first women to earn the *laurea* from *La Sapienza* in Hebrew studies. The *laurea* is a four-year general degree with two more years of specialization. Cavalletti's specialization was in "The Philology, Culture and History of Ancient Eastern Semitic Languages." The degree required a thesis and the *laureati* were usually addressed as *dottore* or in the case of women, like Sofia, as *dottoressa*.

When Zolli died on March 2, 1956, Cavalletti was well on her way to becoming a recognized Hebrew scholar. She was asked to write several of the tributes to "her master" and at least four Zolli-related articles were published that year.[5] One of the articles was a major work of twenty-one pages, which included Zolli's bibliography.

Zolli was remembered again formally with gratitude toward the end of Cavalletti's life when she wrote a background article in Italian for her bibliography. It was published as part of the Talbot School of Theology series about Christian educators, written by Scottie May.[6] Cavalletti referred to the Bible as the book with the greatest influence on her, and to Zolli as the one who opened a new way for her to read it. By this she meant that the Old Testament and the New Testament are about relationships with God, rather than the sacred texts of two competing religions.

She continued to work seriously as a Hebrew scholar, even after her interest in children began, which is apparent in her bibliography. From 1954 to 2005 she published some forty-six technical articles and seven books in the field of Hebrew studies, including translations of Esther and Leviticus. She was an assistant for Hebrew and Semitic languages at the University of Rome until 1954, but from then on she emphasized her work at the *Centro di Catechesi del buon Pastore* (the Catechetical Center of the Good Shepherd) in Rome, while quietly pursuing her biblical studies.

Cavalletti's five books in the field of Christian education include two privately published for her students at the *Centro*, as well as articles and chapters in books. Her book with the greatest influence among English speaking readers is *The Religious Potential of the Child.*[7]

The Influence of Montessori

Montessori's influence was a surprise! It began in the spring of 1954, the same year that Zolli's autobiography was published and Cavalletti was an aspiring young Hebrew scholar. Two years after the death of Maria Montessori and two years before Zolli's death, a friend brought her son to Sofia for some lessons about religion. They were soon joined by two other children.[8]

The Cavalletti family was Roman Catholic. Sofia had been given a firm foundation centered around the Mass, which was very fortunate, because in those days Roman Catholic education for children consisted mostly of memorizing the catechism, questions and answers in abstract, adult language. As a child she found this exercise to be empty and sterile, despite her quick wit and powerful memory, so she knew she didn't want to do *that* with her new young friends. She merely opened the Bible, which she loved, and they talked about God.

Cavalletti's interest and ability as a teacher of children did not go unnoticed by the experienced and energetic Adele Costa Gnocchi, who was known to the Cavalletti family. Sofia had first visited her Montessori school, which had no name, when she was a teenager.

The formidable Costa Gnocchi had been born in Montefalco in 1883 and was a champion of children's education and women's rights. She was known merely as "La Signorina" (The Unmarried Woman), who was too busy to be married. She had attended Montessori's first training course in 1909 and founded her school in Rome in 1919 in the Palazzo Taverna, not far from the Cavalletti home.

During World War II Costa Gnocchi's school was saved from the Fascist police by its anonymity and by being hidden behind the walls of the old *palazzo*. Mussolini closed all the Montessori schools in Italy and jailed some of the teachers, but Costa Gnocchi told the police that the school was her private study. No one gave away the secret and children continued to come and go.

When Montessori returned from India after World War II, she and Costa Gnocchi began to study and experiment with children from birth to three years of age. They discovered that the Montessori environment for children from three to six was inappropriate for these younger children, so they designed a special environment that they called "*il nido*" (the nest). From this collaboration came the Assistants to Infancy course, begun in 1948, with training now around the world. Costa Gnocchi was also a *Docente di Filosofia*, a recognized university teacher of philosophy, but not on the regular staff. It was *this* brilliant, energetic, and imposing woman who persuaded Cavalletti to teach religion to children and introduced her to Gianna Gobbi, her life-long collaborator.

Gianna had begun to work at Costa Gnocchi's school as a teenager. Costa Gnocchi was always on the lookout for talented teachers and had noticed Gianna's gift. This gift was affirmed when Maria Montessori presented her last course in Rome in 1951. Gianna was chosen to be her assistant.

The special capacity of Gianna Gobbi to relate to children became legendary. She was not tall, so it was easy to look children in the eye. She had a ready smile, a wonderful sense of humor, and bright, sparkling eyes. The mother of a child taught by Gianna at the *Centro*, who herself had been taught by Gianna, said at Gianna's funeral in 2002 that "she smiled like a little girl" and took children "quite seriously with the intelligence of the mind and of the heart." She remembered experiencing the collaboration between Cavalletti and Gobbi as if Gianna took children by the hand and brought them to the Word of God. It was Sofia's task to bring the Word of God to the children.[9]

Gobbi's contribution to the collaboration can also be seen in her *Listening To God with Children: The Montessori Method Applied to the Catechesis of Children*.[10] This book was developed and translated in a two-step process in 1992 and 1998, finally coming under the care of Rebekah Rojcewicz for its completion. Gobbi's Montessori training was limited to early childhood, but the basic principles of the Montessori approach were well understood from deep reflection and long experience, so she and Cavalletti worked out together how to engage children in middle and late childhood.

Gobbi and Cavalletti began to meet with children in the Cavalletti home at 34 Via Degli Orsini soon after they were introduced to each other. This is an address familiar to all those who made the pilgrimage to see Sofia over the decades. It became the site of the *Centro* and is a spacious, high ceilinged, Renaissance space with ample room for three large classrooms, as well as a large area for Sofia to live comfortably and provide for her live-in maid. Cavalletti and Gianna worked with a host of talented and dedicated colleagues to guide children's spiritually until their deaths, but we are running ahead of our story.

In 1957 Cavalletti was asked to give a paper at an International Montessori Congress in Rome. This introduced her to Montessorians around the world. In 1958 the international scope of her work was enlarged by a trip to Dublin to give a course for teachers. Her later visits to the United States, Canada, Mexico, Germany, Greece, and elsewhere expanded the world's awareness of what she and her colleagues had discovered at the center in Rome.

In 1959 Signorina Gobbi also began to teach in the *Scuola Assistenti all'Infanzia* (Assistants to Infancy School) in Rome. Her specialty had always been with children from about three through six years, but this gave her a chance to begin working with infants. She taught primarily with Dr. Silvana Montanaro, a psychiatrist in Rome, who established the *Association Montessori Internationale* (AMI) Assistants to Infancy Course. Dr. Montanaro also helped Cavalletti and Gobbi with the development of the Catechesis of the Good Shepherd.

The year 1959 was an important one in Rome. Pope John XXIII announced the Second Vatican Council on January 25th. "Standing before you I tremble somewhat with emotion but am humbly resolute in my purpose to proclaim a twofold celebration: a diocesan synod for the city of Rome, and a general Council for the universal Church."[11] No one expected this, so the city was buzzing. Roncalli was supposed to be a transition pope, but the old pontiff, nearly eighty years old, was full of surprises. He opened the proceedings by saying, "The council now beginning rises in the Church like daybreak, a forerunner of the most splendid light. It is now only dawn."

During the late 1950s and early 1960s there was also a great deal of creative ferment at the *Centro*. Cavalletti, Gobbi, and the children were shifting the emphasis for teaching about the Mass from the sacrifice of Christ toward the Good Shepherd gathering "sheep" around his table. As she once said to me, and probably to others, "It took me almost twenty years to discover this."

It was also during this period that in 1961 Cavalletti and Gobbi published their first book *Educazione religiosa, liturgia e metodo Montessori* (Religious Education, Liturgy and the Montessori Method). It was translated into English in 1964 with the misleading title *Teaching Doctrine and Liturgy*.

The book began by tracing the history of Montessori religious education and then described the work at the Center. Cavalletti made special mention of the educator and former army officer Michel Lanternier's work in France. He organized the life of his school in Rennes around the Mass and the liturgical year. Cavalletti gratefully acknowledged other sources. In Standing's *The Child in the Church* she would also mention that some of her work in Rome "has been copied from the Dominican Sisters at the Sion Hill Convent, Blackrock, Dublin—and from other material devised by members of the Catholic Montessori Guild in England."[12]

In 1963 an international organization, *L'Associazione "Maria Montessori" per la formazione religiosa del bambino* (The Maria Montessori Association for the Religious Formation of the Child) was founded. Today the pioneering work of Cavalletti and Gobbi guides a growing, world wide network. *L'Associazione* was fifty years old in 2013.

The Catechesis of the Good Shepherd

Io sono il buon pastore (I Am the Good Shepherd) was published in 1970–1971 for several age levels.[13] It was a beautiful curriculum with strong, contemporary illustrations, a simple clear text, and with teaching guides for the teachers. It provides a good summary of Cavalletti's approach, but it is also an anomaly. It was decided not to publish the Catechesis of the Good Shepherd as a curriculum but to move forward in the classical Montessori way of putting the theory in books and keeping the training in an oral tradition. This was because the spiritual formation of teachers is deeply personal. They make their own notebooks (as in Montessori) and construct their own materials (unlike Montessori).

The book that made Cavalletti and Gobbi's work known in the United States was *The Religious Potential of the Child: The Description of an Experience with Children from Ages Three to Six*. It described Cavalletti's "method of signs." A sign, like a butterfly, is destroyed when it is pinned to a board for analysis and classification. The wings are still there but it cannot fly. The way to keep signs alive is to show children how to meditate on them. An invitation to meditate is not like asking children to enter into a private flight of fantasy. It is an invitation for the child to enter more deeply into reality, such as the transformation of seeds into growing grain or the rising of dough after leaven has been added. These are much more than literary analogies. They invite meditation on the reality of life itself!

As Cavalletti said about meditating on parables:

> In order to pierce the meaning of the parable we need to work with our imagination and our intuition. We need to use our imagination because we must not move away from the images through which the parable reveals reality to us. The author of the parable has not worked with fantasy; the likeness he is suggesting to us between the two levels of reality is not his own personal creation, nor is it a literary contrivance; it is an ontological likeness: The Kingdom of God can be compared to a mustard seed because the seed *is* in some way a bearer of the reality of the Kingdom.[14]

This approach does not teach the answers to life's theological questions, despite a single "theological point" assigned to each lesson. Cavalletti sometimes smiled about this and, waving her finger in a Roman way, said to me, mischievously,

"There are many points, you know." What is actually taught is her method of signs.

Signs, such as the parables, are peripheral to the center, where the relationship with God is allowed to remain the child's own. "Slowly, as we go deeper into the heart of things by concentrating on one point, we will come to realize, with infinite wonder, that the global vision of reality becomes always greater."[15] A single parable, if gone into deeply enough, can open up the child's relationship to the infinity of God.

A comparison between Cavalletti's adaptation of the "center and the periphery" model and the one used in general Montessori education will help. Standing described this as follows:

> We have, then, these two aspects of the child's work: (1) an outer, motor activity at the periphery of the personality; and (2) accompanying this, a profound, invisible, creative process at the center. About this latter the teacher need not worry. It will look after itself. Her business is to feed the periphery by presenting and explaining the various occupations which are the means to development. Once she has stimulated this peripheral activity, the directress can, and should, retire, secure in the knowledge that if she interferes at this stage she will only be retarding, instead of assisting development.[16]

"Feeding of the periphery" in general Montessori education involves presenting many different kinds of lessons to help children discover an essential reality or skill. The many lessons used to demonstrate borrowing and carry-over are an example. These range from the golden beads, to the stamp game, to the abacus, and to other materials. Once the child "gets it" at the center of his or her experience, the observer can see that the child is no longer interested in the sensorial materials that led to the discovery. This is because the child has moved on toward abstraction and mastery.

In religious education the stimulus at the periphery is different. This can be illustrated by thinking about the many lessons Cavalletti and Gobbi developed about the Mass. Working with those lessons the children get involved but do not move away from the relationship with God at the center. Each lesson takes them deeper into the relationship with God from a different perspective provided by the Mass. What they discover is not a skill or an abstraction but a perspective on their relationship with God at the center. Feeding the periphery helps them settle more deeply into this relationship, as it grows silently and invisibly like a seed. This is why the various details of the Mass can be meditated on for a lifetime.

Maria Montessori's experiments focused on the Mass and other liturgical practices. Cavalletti added the Bible. It was her interest and training in scripture combined with Gianna's observations of children that convinced them that children needed to encounter and respond to God through the Bible as well as the liturgy.

For example, the parables are worked with in pairs. One child moves stand-up, wooden figures, such as the Good Shepherd and the sheep, while the other child reads the parable from a little booklet. Cavalletti wrote, "Such figures were presented in a more or less abstract manner in order to differentiate them from the figures used in the Christmas or Easter panorama, since these latter stand for definite historical persons."[17]

Cavalletti's experiments with the parables were the stimulus for the section of parable shelves in the Godly Play room, which include the guiding parables from the synoptic gospels with one "I Am" statement from John in gold boxes on the top shelf. Parables about parables, sayings, and the synthesis lesson as well as other teaching objects are kept on the shelves below. Keeping the parables in their own shelf section helps distinguish them from the teaching objects on the sacred story shelves and the liturgical shelves. Parables in Godly Play are usually two-dimensional and lie flat on the underlay. Sacred stories are usually three-dimensional, and liturgical materials are a combination of two-dimensional and three-dimensional objects. These distinctions are to help children distinguish and talk about the different genres in the Christian language system as they get older.

Cavalletti and Gobbi also used Montessori's idea of the *spiral* curriculum, which Godly Play uses, but they wind it more tightly. They defined the indirect preparation and direct preparation for each lesson as well as the direct aims and indirect aims with explicit doctrinal points for each lesson. Godly Play is more flexible.

While Cavalletti and Gobbi were at work quietly and patiently with the children in Rome there was a larger revolution in Roman Catholic religious education brewing that also influenced their work and gave it a larger context. This shift of perspective began in 1936, completely unknown to Sofia, who was about nineteen at the time.

The Austrian Jesuit Josef Andreas Jungmann published *Die Frohbotschaf und unsere Glaubensverkundigung* (The Good News and our Proclamation of Belief). The first response from Rome was to have the book immediately withdrawn from publication. There was a sense in Rome that this proposal challenged the sole authority of the Magisterium, made up of the pope and bishops, to interpret the faith. The interpretation of the Bible by the faithful was a sensitive issue, since that is the issue the Reformation raised. Salvation history as a means to interpret scripture was not formally accepted until Vatican II.

Jungmann's proposal was serious and Rome knew this. He was a great liturgical scholar who felt compelled to write about religious education. He urged the church to move beyond the scholastic-laden catechism approach inherited from previous centuries, and argued that children needed to hear the announcement of Christ's birth, death, and resurrection (*kerygma*) and to see a vision of how their lives fit into the history of salvation. The words "liturgy," "proclamation," and "salvation history" became key terms and themes in Cavalletti's educational approach.[18]

Two books Cavalletti prepared for her two-year long courses in Rome demonstrate the influence of this revolution on her work. *La storia della Salvezza* (The History of Salvation) and *Corso di Liturgia* (The Flow of the Liturgy), were published privately, but the Catechesis of the Good Shepherd organization in the United States translated the two books with new titles: *History's Golden Thread* and *Living Liturgy*. They were translated and edited by two of Cavalletti's early students in Rome, Patricia A. Coulter and Rebekah Rojcewicz, with the help of others. They are but two of the many resources that Catechesis of the Good Shepherd has graciously made available in English.

While this revolution in Roman Catholic education was taking place the work in the *Centro* continued. In 1996 a loose confederation of national organizations was set up. They were linked by the *Consiglio* (Council), which gathers every three years. At least seven countries have associations that send representatives, but over thirty-seven countries are now involved in some way with the Catechesis of the Good Shepherd.

The Catechesis of the Good Shepherd (CGS) organization in the United States was founded in the summer of 1983 and incorporated in 1986. It is part of the *Consiglio* and is a well-established, smoothly running organization that provides resources and a directory of Catechesis programs in the United States. It also communicates information about training, does fundraising, and is supportive of both trainers and teachers for their work with children.

As Catechesis expanded world-wide, it became more ecumenical under Cavalletti's leadership. In 1983 the Level I Course in the United States was the first to officially welcome those who were not Roman Catholic. This went a step beyond the first two generations of Montessori religious education.

Gianna Gobbi died in 2002 and Sofia Cavalletti in 2011. The first director of CGS in the United States, Valentina Lillig, known as "Tina," died in 2009. One of the many gifts Tina left was *Catechesis of the Good Shepherd: Essential Realities*. This is a book that brings to life in their own words the "two founding mothers" and others who helped create the Catechesis of the Good Shepherd.[19]

Jerome W. Berryman (1937–)

In 1972 Thea and I arrived in Rome with our daughters, Alyda and Coleen. We were on our way home from a year of studying Montessori in Bergamo, Italy, near Milan. Our girls especially remember riding in the tiny, clattering, impossibly ancient elevator to Sofia's floor. We needed help "to ascend," because Coleen walks with crutches and a brace since she is paralyzed from her chest down from the birth defect spina bifida.

I pressed the bell and Augusta opened the door. She ushered us in and there was Sofia with her aristocratic elegance and natural humility! *Umiltà* and *povertà* were important to her, as they were to *il poverello d'Assisi*, the little poor one, St. Francis. Humility, she often reminded her students, including me, is as important for teachers to be able to truly observe children as it is for adults to work together. It was altogether fitting that in 1997 an international retreat took place in Assisi to celebrate her work with Gianna. This was the last time I saw Sofia, but again I am jumping ahead in the story. Let's return to a quarter of a century earlier in Rome.

Augusta served coffee and we began our visit in Italian, talking with happy animation, amid the paintings, books, and family photographs in Sofia's study. Her well-worn Hebrew Bible was open on her desk. Outside the window was the famous clock tower with a small piazza in front of it, the *Piazza dell'Orologio*. After a short time Sofa suggested that we change to English and mentioned discreetly that *our girls* spoke Italian with a North Italian accent.

How did the little boy who was playing in his grandmother's yard as this book began find his way to Rome? It is worth taking a moment to answer this question, because in 1991 Sofia and I sat in the very same room and talked about the differences between Godly Play and Catechesis of the Good Shepherd. Part of that discussion was about how we came from very different backgrounds.

When I was about five I spent the night with my Grandmother Cauthers. As I was about to go to sleep, it seemed like the whole side of the house fell away and I looked out into an enormous empty space. This boundless emptiness pressed against but also pulled at me. I cried out, "I don't want to die." In the dark my grandmother's voice comforted me, but it seemed she was speaking for someone larger or something beyond her, perhaps the Power I knew but had no name for.

The God of Power was known by presence, not absence. It was everywhere as I played, watched things grow, saw puppies being born, and buried my dogs among the lilac bushes when they died. The Church God was something else. You had to go to the brick church with the square bell tower to find that kind of power, which seemed somehow domesticated. People got dressed up to go there. It was not like playing outside in the grass and trees. Everything was quiet and polite, but it was nice to be there among the stained glass stories in the windows and the wooden arches. There was strange furniture there to think about, things we didn't have at home.

One Easter Sunday after the usual roast beef, carrots, and potatoes at Grandmother Berryman's a multitude of uncles and aunts with their children gathered in the huge vegetable garden out behind the barn. The sun was bright and warm after the dark and cold of winter. We children ran and played along the rows of sprouting growth, weaving in and out among the grown-ups. You could feel the energy of life everywhere, blending with the Easter things that had been said, sung, and done in the church. The God of Power and the Church God came together that day for me, but this was a private intuition. I did not have the words to say it to anyone and besides I wasn't sure I wanted to try. Let me explain.

Sunday school was in the basement of the church. We gathered together for "opening exercises," then we divided into age groups and were led to smaller rooms. I remember sitting at a curved table around the teacher. The teacher talked. We colored. Before leaving we memorized the Bible verse for the day. Once, when my parents asked what I learned in Sunday school, I answered confidently, "He eats carrots for me." They laughed. I was ashamed, but that *was* the memory verse for the day. Why the laughter? I had the theology all worked out. I hated carrots. Anyone who would eat carrots for me was truly special! It was such a person who was always being talked about in church. The actual verse, "He careth for me," made much less sense.

It was my senior year in high school before I ventured out again publicly into the theological world. I was asked to teach a class of rambunctious boys in our Presbyterian church on Sunday mornings. My younger brother and cousins were the most skilled at disturbance, but I had an authority little boys could respect. I averaged three touchdowns a game in football, a little over eighteen points a game in basketball, and was the undefeated state champion in the low hurdles. This did not solve all the behavior problems, however, but I too had been disruptive, so I knew all the tricks and they knew I knew. This experience helped me realize that I could "teach religion" and that it was important somehow for me to do this and to keep trying to do this well.

I went to the University of Kansas to play basketball and run track (and study history and literature on the side), but I blew my knee apart stepping down over a high hurdle and went from being fast to barely walking. I had to reconstruct my life from the ground up, so I moved on to Princeton Theological Seminary to continue my spiritual quest.

We studied and talked theology in the classes at Princeton, but more importantly Karl Barth visited the campus and I discovered that he smiled and had an astounding sense of humor. In the evenings there were seriously boisterous seminars with Sam Keen about philosophy, which made the ideas vibrate with potency. Sam was working on his Ph.D. about the French existentialist Gabriel Marcel at the University and helped bring Marcel to the seminary to give a lecture. At McCarter Theater I got to hear Carl Sandburg, Robert Frost, E.E. Cummings and others read their poetry. Gerhard von Rad came for a year from Germany to teach Old Testament and salvation history. As the quest continued, my job at the information desk of the YMCA each evening helped me keep my balance and to see another side to living in Princeton.

Most importantly, however, was the day I saw a girl walking down Nassau Street with her long braid swinging behind her. She danced along in her black leotard and a short, Scottish kilt. My bland world burst into color. Thea was a dancer, studying voice at Westminster Choir College in Princeton. We discovered that we loved each other and loved children. We didn't know much about what that meant yet, but *we knew enough*. The third year we were married and lived in a little cottage on the edge of an estate near Princeton, while still going to school. She worked as the housekeeper and I was the groundskeeper.

In *The Religious Potential of the Child* Cavalletti wrote: "In helping the child's religious life, far from imposing something that is foreign to him, we are responding to the child's silent request: 'Help me to come closer to God by myself.'"[20] I understood this intuitively from my own growing up, which pushed me towards theology, but when I took the required class in Christian education at Princeton I learned that I did not know *how* to help children come closer to God by themselves. What we were being taught to teach children was the opposite, which was to explain rather than show how. Explaining seemed to block self-discovery and take away children's spiritual integrity and initiative. This conflict stimulated a search for a better way, which began in 1960. Cavalletti and Gobbi had already been at work with children in Rome for six years by that time and were preparing their first book for publication, but I knew nothing about this.

From 1965 to 1968 I was a chaplain at Culver Military Academy in northern Indiana. I had attended Culver in the summers. My father and uncle had also been summer students at this beautiful boarding school with a strong athletic program and a long tradition of great teaching. In addition to being a chaplain I helped coach basketball and track, which healed that interrupted part of my life. I also taught history, poetry, and religion. This affirmed that I loved teaching, but I also intuited that adolescence was rather late in the game for building fundamental spiritual foundations. This and the arrival of our two girls turned my attention to the religious lives of children.

It was also during this time that I learned in an indelible way that young children are aware of the limits to knowing and being. Coleen had just been born and Thea was still in the hospital. I sat in our living room to tell Alyda, Coleen's older sister who had been staying with friends, about Coleen's complex birth. Alyda was about five years old and perched on the edge of what seemed like an impossibly huge couch. She watched intently as I struggled with what to say. Finally, she asked, "Is Mommy dead?" That was her existential question. The next morning I baptized Coleen in the back of the ambulance and we drove the length of Indiana to James Whitcomb Riley Hospital in Indianapolis to begin Coleen's care and wonderful life with us.

After three years we moved to Tulsa, where I finished law school and passed the bar. Soon afterwards Thea and I were sitting in the observation room of a Montessori school, watching our girls moving about as they learned. That was it! That was the method for Christian education I was looking for! We moved to Italy to learn more.

During Godly Play's first decade of development, 1974 to 1984, I worked in schools, churches, and in the Texas Medical Center in Houston. Two events took place that helped crystallize the shape of Godly Play. The first took place while working on an interdisciplinary team at Houston Child Guidance

Center studying families with suicidal children. These families did not tell stories about births, deaths, grandparents, vacations, the parents' childhoods, or any other key experiences or people in the life of the family. They had no narrative. I had come from a storytelling family, so I was stunned that people could live like that. What I learned was that they really *could not* live like that, at least their children could not. That is why they were intent on suicide.

Part of the treatment was to get the families to tell stories. When they did this the children got better, which seemed to indicate that storytelling, along with the other treatment modalities, was critical. This experience moved me back to the parish to be sure that the Great Story got told to children. What had seemed so simple in my growing up turned out to be absolutely fundamental to being an authentic human being.

The second event summed up my ten years in the Texas Medical Center. I presented a paper at a conference at M.D. Anderson, the great cancer hospital in the TMC. It was called "The Chaplain's Strange Language: A Unique Contribution to the Health Care Team."[21] The paper described how the Christian language domain differed from and yet could work together with the domain of science. I had been living and working in this interplay for a decade. The first people who truly saw what Godly Play could do for children were the child-life workers at Texas Children's Hospital, because they had felt the limitations of the domain they worked in for helping children cope with the limits to their being and knowing. It is hard to pretend that children are not aware of their existential limits in a pediatric hospital.

I had continued to correspond with Sofia Cavalletti during these years, but it was impossible for me to go to Rome for two years for her training course. Instead, I organized an international training course for her to come to Houston in 1978. This was my first training in the Catechesis of the Good Shepherd and Cavalletti's second course in the United States.

The Interplay of Catechesis of the Good Shepherd and Godly Play: Founders and Followers, Once Again

By 1991 my relationship with Sofia was at its midpoint. We had met in 1971 when she came north from Rome to Bergamo to lecture during my training to be a Montessori teacher. By 1991 we had known each other for twenty years. It would be another twenty years before she died in 2011.

During the first half of our relationship she was my mentor. It was good, however, that my mentor lived on the other side of the Atlantic Ocean. This gave Thea and me room to make our own discoveries from our weekly encounters with children. We worked directly with children on Sundays in various churches and on Saturdays we held two-hour research classes, one in the morning for young children and another in the afternoon for older children.

Sofia's letters and continuing example nourished and challenged me, but Thea's and my direct experience with children in Montessori schools, in churches, in hospitals, and in our research classes was moving us in a different direction. Sofia sensed this independence. One day, during one of my early visits to Rome, she remarked in passing that I was a "good Montessori child." By this she meant that I needed to find my own way.

Sofia may have thought at first that I might play a larger role in the development in her work and organization. I thought so, too. We met with Luigi C. Capogrossi and others in her study one day during the 1980s to discuss this. I had come to Rome to study with Cavalletti and had given a lecture at a *libreria* near the Vatican, which Sofia had arranged. During the meeting in her study I asked, "But what would I do?" She replied, "It is not a question of what but of whom."

It was during that visit that I began to think more clearly about what I already suspected: Thea and I were, indeed, moving in our own direction. When I returned to Rome in 1991 it was obvious that what we were doing in Houston no longer fit within the frame of the Catechesis of the Good Shepherd, even though we shared the same Montessori tradition. My book *Godly Play*[22] had just been published, so what we were doing even had a different name.

I arrived in Rome during November to study with Sofia for a month and to observe her classes. I also wanted to work in her library to bring her bibliography up to date and to take a more systematic look at her Center for Documentation. A grant from Lilly Endowment funded the trip.

During this visit, I stayed at the *Casa Santa Maria*, near the Trevi Fountain, with the Roman Catholic priests from North America, who were doing graduate work in the great pontifical institutes of Rome. Out the back door of the *Casa* was the Pontifical Biblical Institute, called the "Biblicum," where Sofia had once studied. At the far end of the Piazza della Pilotta was the Pontifical Gregorian University, where Zolli had taught and prayed.

Toward the end of that rainy month, Sofia and I sat down with Carol Dittberner, a Catechesis of the Good Shepherd teacher and trainer from the United States. Carol had trained with Sofia in 1974 in St. Paul, the first time she came to the United States, so she had known Sofia almost as long as I had.

Carol tape-recorded Sofia's and my discussions on 21–22 November about the relationship between Godly Play and Catechesis. A document was then prepared at the request of the Association in Rome to clarify the likenesses and differences in our work. A copy of this two-page memorandum is in the archives of the Center for the Theology of Childhood in Denver. It was called "A Conversation in Rome."

Five likenesses were listed first. We both considered our work unfinished. We both shared a deep respect for the spirituality of children and were taking great care to support the child's relationship with God. We both arrived at our "common consciousness," coming from "different backgrounds, each having the child as our guide." We both followed "the principles of the Montessori method by providing an environment especially prepared for the religious life of the child." This setting is a place with "an atmosphere of recollection which can be leading to meditation and prayer." Finally, for both of us "concrete materials are used to aid the child's work."

Some key differences were also listed. First, the parables were not treated in quite the same way. We both presented "The Good Shepherd," "The Mustard Seed," "The Great Pearl," and "The Leaven" to children from three to six years old. In addition Sofia presented "The Hidden Treasure" and "The Corn Seed" while I presented "The Sower" and "The Good Samaritan." Nothing was said about *the way the parables were presented*, which also differs, and nothing was mentioned about the parable synthesis lesson for older children in Godly Play or the description of the Christian language system, which places the parables in context. The intent of the document was to keep the differences clear and concise but general and to focus on the practicalities. After all, we had both affirmed that neither

Catechesis of the Good Shepherd nor Godly Play should be considered "finished."

The second difference noted was our respective approaches to "the Old Testament." Sofia began with "one global history of Salvation" placing the emphasis on "the unity of history" and the moments of Creation, Redemption, and Parousia that give shape to that unity. After the children were grounded in this awareness, she moved to "specific events in Scripture" and introduced the Old Testament from six years on; although in practice, it seemed from my observations that this was usually later during middle childhood or in late childhood.

Godly Play, on the other hand, began at the beginning with the Hebrew Scriptures at age three with the first story of God's creation in Genesis and moved by means of the narrative toward the part that is not yet finished. The emphasis in Godly Play is on the people of God seeking God's elusive presence. Any common themes in the Hebrew or Christian Scriptures are left for the children to discover.

Cavalletti emphasized salvation history, proclamation (*kerygma*), and the connection to history through the liturgy. These were exciting ideas that were in the air during Vatican II in Rome. Godly Play relied more on the truth being embodied in the experiences the narrative is based than on concepts. Cavalletti, as she had told me earlier, was also concerned that children need to know that they are Christians before introducing the Hebrew Scriptures. This is a valid concern, but the children in Houston did not seem to be worried or concerned about this. They let the story unfold and intuited how stories, parables, and liturgical acts from long ago were still alive today and helpful to guide their own longing to follow God's elusive presence in their lives. They literally grasped this meaning with their hands as they worked with the teaching materials and wondered together in community and in small groups or individually through their art responses.

The source for Godly Play's biblical theology is Samuel Terrien's *The Elusive Presence*[23] rather than the salvation history school. This approach emphasizes the experience of God's presence. Questions about whether the New Testament is the completion of the Old Testament, is its replacement, or has an independent status do not come up, because God's presence is presented in narrative form rather than abstractions and because experiencing God is not under anyone's control, Jewish or Christian. Children know this from their own experiences of God's presence in their lives. What they need to make meaning from this experience is the coherence of a room full of stories, parables, and liturgical action that embody the whole system of Christian language to help them give voice to what they know. With God's help and this powerful language they can then more fully respect what they have experienced, use it to make meaning, and evaluate it. The emphasis in Godly Play is on inviting children into Christian language rather than proclaiming it to them.

The third contrast mentioned in "A Conversation in Rome" was about the teaching of liturgy. Cavalletti did much more direct and detailed teaching about Holy Communion, which has merit. Godly Play places the same emphasis on liturgical acts but does so by providing a long line of presentations about worship beginning with the organization of the Tabernacle in the Hebrew Scriptures to a model worship setting for labeling and moving the objects while tracing the steps in formal Christian worship. Godly Play is more indirect and uses more narrative and discovery in its teaching about liturgical action than Catechesis.

The final difference mentioned was about the "structure of the children's meetings." Sofia's approach was more flexible. The classes at the *Centro* were two hours long, while Godly Play was developed intentionally within the parish setting for Sunday mornings when classes are limited to one hour. The research classes for Godly Play, however, were always two hours long, because it takes time for children to become deeply involved, to relax, and to move through several pieces of work. Sunday morning is definitely a compromise between the spiritual needs of the children and the needs of the adult schedule. Godly Play, however, provides strategies to help make this adaptation work for the children.

Regardless of the time involved, however, Godly Play's process follows the deep structure of the Holy Eucharist. *It is not the Holy Eucharist,* but it includes the whole structure to provide an indirect preparation for Christian worship. A second reason for this structure is that it is the way the Christian people have prayed together since the early church, so it has proven to be the best way to learn the language for creating existential meaning in the church community. This whole process combines the Liturgy of the Word (the lessons and responses) and the Liturgy of Holy Communion (sharing the feast and its prayers).

The document memorializing our conversation concluded by saying that it took place in Rome 21–22 November, 1991, and was tape recorded by Carol Dittberner. Sofia and I both signed it. A picture was taken to memorialize this event. The three of us were sitting on a couch in her study. Sofia and Carol sat close together, leaning in one direction, while I sat a bit apart leaning in the other direction. I did not realize at the time how symbolic this photograph was, but after signing this document I felt free to continue developing Godly Play with a good heart.

Sofia summed up our formal and informal conversations over the years by saying that we agreed on so much more than we disagreed that the disagreements were not very important. That remained true for the two of us, which has been very important for me to hold dear. I have nothing but gratitude for Sofia as my mentor because of all she taught me, but the wisdom of having a "conversation in Rome" to send me on my way was, perhaps, her greatest gift.

Sofia and I continued to correspond until her death, but the number of letters and then e-mails declined and focused more on family and friends than religious education. She was busy with the development of her work, busy with the children in Rome, busy with her international organization, and involved in the many friendships with colleagues and followers from all over the world. In the meantime Thea and I continued to explore with children the path we had taken and the development of Godly Play's organization.

When Thea and I went to Rome in November of 2000, Sofia was not able to see us. It was another rainy November and Sofia was eighty-three years old. She did not feel like receiving guests that day, which we understood. Thea and I were eager to see her, but we also just wanted to be in Rome again together and to visit one of the world's most important museums of ancient musical instruments to enrich Thea's teaching in her Montessori music classes. This was our last visit to Rome. Thea was already beginning to suspect the presence of the cancer she was diagnosed with the following July. She died in January of 2009.

Conclusion

Catechesis of the Good Shepherd and Godly Play remain unfinished. We continue to look towards finding better and better ways to help children help themselves to know God. Our church needs this and so does our world, because the capacity for redemptive healing expands as children's spirituality matures and there is much in our world, including ourselves, that needs healing.

4.

Godly Play
and the Center-point

We are now at the book's midpoint. It is time to shift from the past to the present and from the larger Montessori tradition to Godly Play. We will also move from outside to inside, from the people and politics of the tradition to how Godly Play feels. The style will change from narrative to poetry and commentary.

Let's begin with poetry. This chapter is about what T. S. Eliot called the "still point." We will call it "transitional space," "the middle realm" or, as the title of this chapter suggests, "the center-point." It is hard to know what to call it because, as Eliot says, it is a place one can go to and know that one has been there, but cannot say where. This poetry comes from "Burnt Norton," the first long poem in Eliot's *Four Quartets*, one of the most analyzed poems in the English language:

At the still point of the turning world. Neither flesh
  nor fleshless;
Neither from nor towards; at the still point, there the dance is,

But neither arrest nor movement. And do not call it fixity,
Where past and future are gathered. Neither movement
    from nor towards,
Neither ascent nor decline. Except for the point, the
    still point,
There would be no dance, and there is only the dance.
I can only say, there we have been: but I cannot say where.
And I cannot say, how long, for that is to place it in time.

. . . .

Love is itself unmoving.
Only the cause and end of movement,
Timeless, and undesiring
Except in the aspect of time
Caught in the form of limitation
Between un-being and being.
Sudden in a shaft of sunlight
Even while the dust moves
There rises the hidden laughter
Of children in the foliage
Quick now, here, now, always—
Ridiculous the waste sad time
Stretching before and after.[1]

Godly Play mentors need to be able to identify this still
point in their own experience so they can help children find it
by showing it to them rather than by talking about it. It is not
"fixity" as Eliot says. It is dynamic, the source of "the dance."
This is a place where there is "the hidden laughter of children
in the foliage." It is where the creative process dwells, full of

enormous potential, as the Image of God, and it is where classical Christian language needs to be absorbed and activated so it can do what it was created to do.

Concerns like this are not new to the Montessori tradition. As you know, Maria Montessori often spoke about the spiritual nature of the child and the teacher. At the end of her life she concluded in *The Absorbent Mind* that education is not so much teaching with love but participating, as one teaches, in the energy of God, who is love. In the next generation E. M. Standing drew on the term *élan vital* coined by the French philosopher Henri Bergson in his *Creative Evolution*. Standing wrote, "the élan of a Montessori class" is a "precious stream of mental energy," which is "mysterious and constant."[2] Sofia Cavalletti spoke of "joy." I can still see her expansively smiling as she began a teachers' meeting in 1991 after the children had left the *Centro*. "There was a *good feeling* in the Center today," she said, and we nodded our assent, for we too had felt that joy.

I never thought much about trying to say more about how Godly Play *felt* until after Thea died. I didn't have to. We knew what a good class felt like without talking about it. A smile, a touch, or a glance was enough to acknowledge its flow. Besides, Godly Play was about *play* with God and the community of children, so play's definition seemed adequate. Then, one day in New York City this question sneaked up on me and caught me unawares. I was watching a class of adult students in the certificate program for the spiritual guidance of children at General Theological Seminary. The year was 2012.

Cheryl Minor and Rosemary Beales led the practice sessions for this course and I led the integration seminars each day after lunch. Cheryl and Rosemary are Episcopal priests and

Godly Play trainers. Cheryl's Ph.D. thesis studied how Godly Play contributes to children's spiritual wellbeing and Rosemary's D.Min. thesis was about the program she developed for parents at the school, where she is the lower school chaplain. In other words the students were in very good hands, so I let my mind wander as I watched.

Each morning the students began by experiencing the whole Godly Play process. First, they "got ready" before entering the room and then they participated in the lesson, wondering about it together while sitting on the floor in a circle with their mentors. They then got out their "work," a kind of serious play with expressive art, journaling, working with the teaching objects, or other self-selected activities. After this they put their work away and gathered in the circle again to share prayers and a simple feast. Finally, they said a formal "goodbye" and left the room. After taking a break they returned and spent the rest of the rigorous day experiencing lesson after lesson after lesson with only short breaks in between.

After the first day this group began to move with ease in and out of the kind of consciousness that we might call "the middle realm." It is that still point out of which our core creativity comes. We had not talked about this, but they had identified this center-point intuitively, as children do. Between the presentations there was laughter, joking around, teasing, insights, critiques, and sometimes serious tears of discovery. To keep on schedule the storyteller would then pause, look around the circle, smile, and say happily with a sense of humor, "Are you ready?" They knew what she meant and returned to the middle realm, their center-point. What is it? Why is it important? To explore these questions let's return to our original unity as infants.

Our Original Unity

Donald W. Winnicott (1896–1971), an English pediatrician and psychiatrist, discovered a state of mind in infants, something like T. S. Eliot's still point, that he called a "transitional space." It is where the "me" and the "not me" is not yet clearly distinguished. This in-between place begins when the infant realizes that there is more to the world than "me" but the alternative is not yet clear. This awareness opens up when the mother (or other primary caregivers) no longer anticipates each of the child's needs and begins to do "good enough mothering" instead. This is good for both the mother and child, because infants begin to realize that their mothers are somewhat separate. This realization begins the transition towards identifying a world that is solidly "out there."

During this transitional time, spontaneity rules and children do not have to be compliant or assertive. Adults don't challenge their ambivalence about inner and outer or self and other. It is a resting place, enjoyed for itself. Winnicott thought that play, art, religion, and creativity all originate in this kind of consciousness, so it is not a point of "fixity." It is where "the dance" flows out from and where we can return to rest and be renewed as adults.

The unity of infancy begins to be fragmented when children are forced to distinguish what is subjective from what is objective, but this falling apart cannot be avoided. It is our original sin. God is no longer fully present nor authentically whole. Still, distinctions must be made to make our way in the world. We lose something as we gain something in our growing up.

When Winnicott talked about transitional space, he also warned about its misuse. It "widens out" into play, the creativity and appreciation of art, religious feeling, and dreaming, but things can also go very wrong with this "widening out." Transitional space can also be the origin of "fetishism, lying and stealing, the origin and loss of affectionate feeling, drug addiction, the talisman of obsessional rituals, etc."[3] How we care for this middle realm is, therefore, very important and is a primary concern of Godly Play.

There is another feature Winnicott noticed about transitional space that is very important for Godly Play. *Objects* can be invested with the same kind of indeterminate consciousness and energy that transitional space is. He called such objects "transitional objects." During the transitional period infants and young children are not asked to choose whether a favorite blanket, a play-worn toy, or even a thumb is part of them or something independent and outside of them. Transitional objects are alive and yet not quite alive, but this doesn't bother children. Memories of this quality, attached to a few treasured possessions, can continue into adulthood. I can still feel the smooth, satin edge of my blue baby blanket next to the corner of my mouth. But this quasi-living quality given to "things" is not just a matter of treasured memory. We also create transitional objects as adults.

Linus, a character in the cartoon strip *Peanuts* by Charles Schulz, carried his baby blanket everywhere he went. Lucy challenged Linus about what he was going to do with it when he grew up. It was simple. He was going to have it made into a sport coat!

Following Winnicott, we might say that such objects are invested with all the characteristics of transitional space such as being playful, beautiful, religious, and stimulating to our creativity. A sweater worn by a loved one now gone, or a bit of furniture purchased on a radiant day, go far beyond their objective utility. They become "numinous," drawing on the

Latin noun *numen*, which suggests the mystery, power, and terrifying presence of divinity.

The middle realm is the original position, the place we start from, but it also comes and goes in intensity as we mature. It is the space in the midst of the four cardinal points on our relational compass—the relationship with the self, with others, with nature, and with God. It is where we go to regain our balance. It is where existentialist philosophers, such as Gabriel Marcel, have said the mystery of being dwells and our authenticity resides.

The theologian John Macquarrie (1919–2007) talked about the middle realm in terms of "being" and described it as "neither subjective nor objective" but what "holds these two together." Macquarrie cautioned that we can't really talk about this without talking about ourselves and to talk about ourselves we need to talk in terms of what is "self-giving and self-disclosing" to us.[4] The wholeness of our relationship with God, self, others, and nature can be fractured by words, but it can also be rediscovered and held together by words. This is the task of classical Christian language and why it is so important to begin giving this gift to children as young as possible as part of the middle realm.

Throughout most of the history of theology the still point in children has been overlooked, but two very great Roman Catholic theologians of the last generation who brilliantly disagreed on many things agreed on the value of the child's original unity. Karl Rahner wrote about original grace being as strong as original sin in his "Ideas for a Theology of Childhood."[5] Hans Urs von Balthasar went further. He argued that children, *including Jesus*, know God in an undifferentiated way through their mother's smile. His last book, *Unless You Become Like This Child*,[6] developed this idea, but his whole theology was centered on God's presence in the mother's smile, which grounded his thought in a reality rather than an abstraction.[7]

This means that original sin is neither discounted nor ignored in Godly Play. It is assumed and can be seen at work in the open classroom full of children moving about with their mentors. But the Godly Play room is also a place filled with the reality of original grace. As children absorb and activate Christian language they obtain the means to continue exploring their fragmentation and personal unity with the Creator all their days.

Godly Play Materials as Transitional Objects

One of the first things many people notice about the Godly Play room is that it is full of teaching objects sitting on shelves. It is hard to know what to call them. Sometimes they are called, rather inelegantly, "manipulables" because they can be manipulated. Sometimes they are called "concrete materials," but they have nothing to do with concrete. Sometimes, as in Montessori, they are called "sensorial materials" to distinguish them from books, maps, posters, and other teaching aids more connected to the eyes than a combination of all our senses. These teaching objects provide a way for Christian language to be literally grasped by the knowing of the body by the senses as well as by the knowing of the mind by reason and the knowing of the spirit by contemplation. To be fully effective, however, they need to be appreciated by the children and their mentors with a love that gives them life and engages the whole person in a pervasive way, somewhat like transitional objects.

To say that teaching materials for Christian education ought to be treated like transitional objects sounds a little strange. I certainly do not mean that one needs to be infantile, childish, or immature to do Godly Play. What I am suggesting is the opposite. One needs to be mature enough to respect the teaching objects so they can have a life of their own. What would that be like?

Rather than providing a description or analysis about how Godly Play teaching materials can be like transitional objects, let's ask Margery Williams to *help us imagine* what it would be like *to be* a transitional object. Her call to the imagination about this was in *The Velveteen Rabbit*, which was published in 1922. It invites us into a somewhat Victorian nursery, where the Velveteen Rabbit and the Old Skin Horse are discussing what is real:

> Real isn't how you are made," said the Skin Horse. "It's a thing that happens to you. When a child loves you for a long, long time, not just to play with, but REALLY loves you, then you become Real."
>
> "Does it hurt?" asked the Rabbit.
>
> "Sometimes," said the Skin Horse, for he was always truthful. "When you are Real you don't mind being hurt."
>
> "Does it happen all at once, like being wound up," he asked, "or bit by bit?"
>
> "It doesn't happen all at once," said the Skin Horse. "You become. It takes a long time. That's why it doesn't happen often to people who break easily, or have sharp edges, or who have to be carefully kept. Generally, by the time you are Real, most of your hair has been loved off, and your eyes drop out and you get loose in the joints and very shabby. But these things don't matter at all, because once you are Real you can't be ugly, except to people who don't understand."[8]

Later the Velveteen Rabbit kept a little boy company during his serious illness. It was not easy but it was important to be there, even if his shape was mostly hugged away, because the child needed him. When the child recovered, the rabbit was gathered up with some books, stuffed in a sack, and thrown out by the grownups. The doctor said the bunny was "a mass of scarlet fever germs" and had to be burned at once. "What? Nonsense! Get him a new one. He mustn't have that anymore!"

Out by the "fowl-house" the Velveteen Rabbit felt lonely, then he noticed that the bag had been left untied. He wriggled out, but "was shivering a little, for he had always been used to sleeping in a proper bed, and by this time his coat had worn so thin and threadbare from hugging that it was no longer any protection to him."

Toward the end of the book, it is as if Margery Williams turns to the adult reader with a question. "Did the Velveteen Rabbit become 'real' for you?" If a tolerable or tentative, "Yes," is offered, she then presses on to imply a larger question. "Can *you* make the transcendent move to become more real, like the Velveteen Rabbit did? Do you have the courage to enter another realm of being?"

If you can feel what this book is about, then you can understand why Godly Play teaching objects need to be beautiful and strong but not over-determined with too many details. This is so they can be loved into the middle realm to connect with the center-point of children as well as adults. If teaching objects are too fussy or mechanical they are emotionally closed and self-contained, so it is hard to love them. If they are not loved then they block the imagination rather than inviting one into the middle realm. This is a little like the efficacy of a cardboard box for play. Children are likely to play longer and with more love and creativity with the box that some shiny new toy came in than the toy itself.

Godly Play materials invite care and respect, as well as opening the door to the imagination and being loved. They are designed to last easily over twenty years, so they can serve many different children and mentors. This gives them plenty of time to be loved into being real. The mentors in the Godly Play room don't *talk* about this to the children, unless there is an emergency that might injure a child or a material. Instead, they *show* how much they value the materials by the way they are touched, carried, cared for, and by the *respectful tone of voice* used when they are referred to and lessons are given. This "tone of voice" is not the silly, sing-song voice sometimes used that demeans the children listening and the adult using it. It is from the heart.

As children sense this respect they learn about the middle realm and how to treat the room and its teaching objects. There is something more they learn, however, that is also very important and is also something to be shown and not just talked about. The children intuit that they too are respected and will be cared for in this place.

This is not a call for silly sentimentalism or childishness. It is a sober plea for being childlike, which is very much connected to the middle realm. The middle realm is not a place where children only do as they please. They need guidance to preserve the gracefulness of this place, so they are given choices from among constructive alternatives. This style of mentoring strikes a meaningful balance between being over-controlling and under-controlling. This is what Montessori was talking about when she wanted teachers to have the objectivity of a scientist and the spirituality of a mystic. This standpoint is like that of an adventurous anthropologist visiting a new culture. The culture of the children in the room needs to be approached as a participant-observer.

The creation of new materials needs the talent of someone who has not lost touch with the middle realm. When this consciousness is missing the objects easily degrade to the status of ordinary toys to be used up and thrown away. The book *Toying with God: The World of Religious Games and Dolls*[9] is a cautionary tale about what can happen in the buying and selling of religious-theme objects as toys. Despite loud marketing that trumpets "kinesthetic learning," "spiritual discovery," and "products" that are designed "to stimulate children's creative imaginations through fun," the objects never quite become real. You can't talk toys into being transitional objects.

The Skin Horse would probably lump the toys reviewed in *Toying with God* with the ones in the nursery that break easily or must be carefully kept. He "had seen a long succession of mechanical toys arrive to boast and swagger, and by-and-by break their main springs and pass away, and he knew that they were only toys, and would never turn into anything else."

Many of the objects reviewed in *Toying with God* are so over-determined and "realistic" that there is no openness for them to be loved and no warmth to invite the child's imagination to engage them. Children will try, of course. They want to play with these toys, but it is frustrating because they do not have the energy of the middle realm to connect with. Sometimes the speech of the dolls and biblical characters is even pre-programmed to utter moral sayings or quote scripture, so the children can't imagine them talking about anything else in their play.

Commercial goals and business competition can bleed the potential life out of such objects. The anti-Barbie dolls are a good example. They were developed for religious reasons to counter the cultural influence and values embodied in Barbie. They still look like Barbie but with slightly changed proportions and, like Barbie, they come with many accessories to sell, which is good business. What is good business, however, promotes materialism, which is supposed to be countered by the toy. It is especially ironic that some of the anti-Barbie dolls were made in the same factory in China where Barbie is manufactured. Over-determination, thinking like one's competitors (religious or economic), and mixing motives (religious and economic) can undermine the best intentions of such manufacturers.[10] The people at Godly Play Resources are well aware of these conflicts, which can't help but arise, so they stay centered. They maintain their balance. They keep their eye on the mission, which is serving the spiritual quest of the children around the world.

Godly Play materials are designed to be obvious and simple without being simplistic and silly. They are not cartoons. Instead, everything that is irrelevant or superficial is trimmed away to leave the heart of the matter. They are spun out of the core metaphor for each sacred story, parable, and liturgical action, so children can discover and enjoy the many levels and angles of meaning waiting for them as they use Godly Play materials in contemplative ways. All this sounds a bit vague. Perhaps an example will help strengthen this assertion. Let's consider the lesson and related materials for "The Ten Best Ways" in Volume 2 of *The Complete Guide To Godly Play*.[11] In the book there are additional details and two illustrations to make this more specific.

Experiencing God's Presence on the Holy Mountain

I wish I could bring you into the Godly Play room that Thea and I built over three decades to present this lesson to you. We really need to have the experience of the lesson and the materials in common before talking about them. St. Gabriel's Episcopal Church in Denver now hosts this room, so children can use it each Sunday. It is part of the Center for the Theology of Childhood with its library nearby, because one can't really study Godly Play by just reading books. One needs to experience it to know it, so with some happy laughter as a fanfare let us proceed with incongruity to read the next few pages about this.

The story takes place in the desert box, which is a box of sand with clear sides so the children can see from their places in the circle what is going on inside the box. A clear lid helps control the interaction with the sand before and after the narrative, since children usually encounter sand with an implied or overt invitation for free play. The sand here, however, is part of this story. It is "the desert" and suggests the harsh wilderness of the Sinai Peninsula. At the same time it points to the vastness of God and God's family by the numberless grains of sand, even in this little "desert." The journey of God's people through this desert is the story of everyone's quest for meaning. We all wander in the desert at times, whatever age we might be.

Sand and spirituality are associated in many parts of the world, but three influences especially guided the use of the sand in this material: Jungian sand play, art therapy, and Navajo sand paintings. The sand paintings of the Navajo people are not like the paintings we hang on the wall. They are a sacred ritual that *invites individuals into the creation* of the traditional sand painting *around them* for their health and guidance. The influence of Jungian sand play and art therapy alerts the mentor to how the sand in the desert box can help externalize unconscious conflicts. The sand is, therefore, more than a metaphor for a historical event. It brings the reality of the event into the present to be experienced, wondered about, and to engage one's unconscious life.

The desert box is placed in the middle of the circle of children. As the story is told the objects representing the People of God, Mt. Sinai, and the Ten Commandments are placed in the desert. Each of the Ten Commandments is written on its own tablet, which looks like a marker for a journey, a gravestone, and part of a heart to indirectly hint at the ultimate nature of these commandments and their relevance to our journey. Placing each commandment on its own tablet makes it easier to move them around in the sand to try out different configurations for exploring how they are related to each other, to us, and to God.

The mountain is crafted to look like the barren mountains in the Sinai Peninsula, so the shape and texture is respectful of the mountain's harshness. The actual shape is similar to the traditional site of Mt. Sinai, so both the children and the adult storyteller can take it seriously. Anyone can Google "Mt. Sinai" today and see pictures of the traditional site, even if it is impossible to go there in person. In Thea's and my Godly Play room we had books and pictures about this traditional site and St. Catherine's Monastery, which is its base.

This "traditional" site added a Christian presence about the third century when Christian hermits lived in caves there, so it is a Christian site today as much as it is a Jewish or Islamic one. In the fourth century Helena, the mother of the Roman emperor Constantine, made a pilgrimage to this place. The Greek Orthodox monastery of St. Catherine, founded in the sixth century, is a treasury of many important, ancient manuscripts, including a letter dated 628 CE from the Prophet Muhammad, signed by an imprint of his hand, since he could neither read nor write. It granted freedom of worship to the monks and "all who adopt

Christianity near and far." Mount Sinai is important to all three of the Abrahamic religions, but, again, in Godly Play a discussion about this is saved for when the children are older, after their grounding in the core story.

In Thea's and my Godly Play room we used a piece of limestone in the shape of the traditional site of Mt. Sinai for our material. It was heavy. Children needed to carry it with two hands or ask older children for help. If dropped it could hurt, but the children in our environment used this material for over thirty years and never dropped it. It was treated with great respect. (The present Godly Play material looks like a barren rock but it is hollow, so if you drop it on your foot there will be no serious consequences. We are, after all, a litigious society.)

The present model is a great improvement over the illustration that accompanies the lesson in the first edition of Volume 2. There has always been pressure on Godly Play Resources to make the model much taller than it is wide. People think that is more impressive. They also want a slot in the top to insert a Moses figure to *proclaim* the Ten Commandments, as if from a tall pulpit. This puts Moses at the center of the event instead of God and implies that the people gathered at the foot of the mountain could see what was going on between God and Moses in the distant, smoky heights. The Godly Play lesson and material, however, are not about the Hollywood version of the story. They are about Moses coming close to God and God coming close to Moses so that Moses mysteriously knew what God wanted him to inscribe on the tablets and deliver to the people.

This approach honors the centuries-old fascination with Moses's encounter with God at Sinai. The Godly Play mentor needs to feel the ancient echoes of this as the lesson is presented. One echo is from the story of the Transfiguration in the gospels

(Matthew 17:1–9, Mark 9:2–8 and Luke 9:28–36). Gregory of Nyssa's *The Life of Moses* represents the Greek Orthodox tradition from the fourth century. One of the most influential texts on the theology of the Middle Ages was written by Pseudo-Dionysius the Areopagite, who lived from the late fifth to the early sixth century. His *Mystical Theology* is an allegory of Moses's ascent up Mt. Sinai. The anonymous spiritual masterpiece called *The Cloud of Unknowing* from the fourteenth century is an early Middle English meditation on this as well. Today this kind of spirituality is still alive. In 1948 Thomas Merton, a Trappist monk, published his autobiographical *The Seven Story Mountain*, which refers to the mountain of Purgatory in Dante's Divine Comedy and adds another dimension to this theme. Finally, during the 1970s Trappist monks such as William Meninger, Basil Pennington, and Thomas Keating began teaching an approach to knowing God from this tradition called "centering prayer," which honors the quest of Moses indirectly, even if the image of ascent and descent fades in favor of "centering." It is this longing for God that the mentor needs to feel, but not commented on, as the Moses figure is moved up and down the mountain.

The Godly Play material includes many figures, as we said. The children are invited to select Moses from the wooden figures in the basket that holds the "People of God" figures. These figures are in various shapes, representing responses to God and each other. They range from exuberance with the arms outstretched to a cautious, perhaps inhibited response with the arms held tightly at the figures' sides. There are both men and women. It is always interesting to watch children working with this lesson alone or in small groups. Which figure will they choose? This is left open so children can play with the question of who Moses really was and what kind of person he might be if he lived today. How would they connect with him? Sometimes children even use a female figure as they reflect on the nature of Moses, which may scandalize some but is deeply meaningful to others.

This openness is in contrast to many people's need to teach a stereotyped figure of Moses in a robe with a beard, staff, and an upraised hand proclaiming "The Ten *Commandments*." This image blocks the children's wonder and exploration of the person, his relationship with God, and the gift from God he made known to us. Children's self identity is also explored in this way, so if we narrow the interpretation of Moses by the way the material is shaped, we also narrow its usefulness to children for their spiritual quest.

After all, how can we know in advance whom the children will identify with in the story? Is it Moses? Perhaps it is the people at the base of the mountain. Is it the desert? What about the mountain itself? Will they make the whole Decalogue or a particular commandment their own? How did people think about Moses after he ascended into the fire and smoke? Did they feel abandoned? A longer version of the story, of course, extends some of these questions, but the basic telling focuses on ascending and descending and implicitly raises these and other wonderings. This is why it is important to take plenty of time to appreciate the difficulty of the climb up through the fire and smoke toward God and the weary return with the tablets.

As the Moses figure slowly climbs upward, the storyteller hides the wooden figure in his or her hand while talking about how it became harder and harder to see him. Finally, he disappears and is completely hidden in the hand or between two hands pressed together like a prayer. The children's attention is directed toward the fire and smoke since Moses is now hidden in the cloud. When Moses starts down the mountain the descent is first traced with a finger and then the hand (or hands) open and Moses can be seen again as he comes close to the people to deliver God's gift.

The Ten Commandments are then placed in the sand with a marker for each one, expressed in essential language that works for both children and adults. As the ten pieces are pressed into the sand they make a pattern to guide our relationships. In the initial presentation one group is about being with God and another is for being with people. "Keeping the Sabbath" is for maintaining both kinds of relationships at the same time. The children, as mentioned above, can also rearrange them in different configurations as they consider their meaning. As they are pressed into the sand they make a satisfying crunch.

The ten tablets are taken out of a red, heart-shaped box and returned to it. This shows that God loves us so much that God gave us—*just gave us*—the ten best ways to live to help us find direction in life and death. These are not the ten-easy-things-to-do. They are all hard, perhaps impossible, but they guide us on our journey today as they did then, like solid markers in the shifting sands of life and death.

Children in early, middle, and late childhood respond to the lesson and materials in different ways. Children in early childhood like the movement of the basic story and are fascinated by the sand. They are concerned about where the story can be found in the room, the texture of the sand, and the lid. They like to move the desert box, which is on wheels.

In middle childhood they wonder more about Moses's encounter with God and the people's encounter with the Decalogue. As children transition into late childhood they challenge the story and the teaching materials as being childish: "We had that lesson already. It's boring." This signals to the mentor that it is time to turn the challenge around and confront the children with the need to find new and deeper meanings in the story and to begin working with the extension lessons such as the one about the life of Moses. But the children need to know *firmly* that this story has challenged people of all ages for well over fifteen centuries. The question, then, is not whether they recognize the story, which is good, but now, *since they are older*, it is time to find new meaning in it at a new level and to recognize that this journey of discovery is one that lasts a lifetime.

With this example of a teaching material in mind we can now turn to a discussion about how such materials help children absorb and activate classical Christian language to make existential meaning and to know God. It is time to talk about the creative process and the making of existential meaning.

The Creative Process and Existential Meaning

The creative process, emerging from the middle realm, is the means to absorb and activate Christian language. We will look at this process from two angles. First, the creative process reveals our affinity with God. Second, although the creative process is used to create new ideas it is also our core identity where God comes to meet us. We will use two guides to explore what it means to create existential meaning with Christian language. One guide is Dorothy L. Sayers and the other one is James E. Loder. For Sayers the climb upwards toward God was enough to know God's presence or "mind." Loder struggled at the edge of the void where God came to meet him.

Dorothy L. Sayers: Coming Close To God

Dorothy L. Sayers published *The Mind of the Maker* in 1941. I first read the 1958 edition, which still makes me smile when I hold it. It only cost $1.35, so it is clearly an *old* friend. Sayers's influence began when I was at Princeton and *The Mind of the Maker* had already taken a central position in Godly Play by the time the research classes began in 1974 at Pines Presbyterian Church in Houston.

Sayers was a widely published creator of novels, detective stories, and plays, which she wrote and helped produce. She was a translator of Dante and had made a living in advertising before becoming successful as an author. She did not suffer fools gladly and was churchwarden at St. Anne's Church, Soho, London for many years, where her ashes were buried beneath the tower.

Dorothy Sayers knew how to create as an author, but she stressed that she was not making up a religion in her book to fit that experience. It was the other way around. Her experience as an author allowed her to make sense out of the creeds, which claim to be stating matters of fact. Her book was neither an argument for Christianity nor an expression of her personal religious belief. It was "a commentary" on the Christian creeds and their claim to be factual.

Since all language is metaphorical, we always know something in terms of something else. "If the word 'Maker' does not mean something related to our human experience of making, then it has no meaning at all."[12] Sayers was no mystic by her own defiant admission, so she was arguing from the way language works, which was something she knew a lot about. Since God created humankind in the Creator's image, the analogy from the human creator to the divine Creator is obvious, but Sayers was not talking about logic. She was talking about a reality that can be experienced factually.

Godly Play is also interested in this reality. When children use the creative process to make meaning with Christian language they are also participating in the Creator's being by their creating. When classical Christian language is absorbed and activated through the creative process, God comes close to children and children come close to God. They are intertwined like a magnificent, invisible braid.

Sayers was "inclined to believe" that the pattern of the creative process "corresponds to the actual structure of the living universe" so if people feel at odds with the universe or powerless in its immensity they are merely stating that they, for whatever reason, are not conforming to the pattern of their true nature. What is that pattern?

> I can only suggest that it is the pattern of the creative mind—
> an eternal Idea, manifested in material form by an unresting
> Energy, with an outpouring of Power that at once inspires,
> judges, and communicates the work; all these three being one
> and the same in the mind and one and the same in the work.
> And this, I observe, is the pattern laid down by the theologians as the pattern of the being of God.[13]

This is why Godly Play is Trinity-centered and God is invited to come and play with the children as they make meaning together with Christian language, the language of grace that came from God through Jesus Christ and can be understood from the depths of original grace in our own being.

James E. Loder: God Coming Close To Us

Our second guide is James E. Loder. His *The Transforming Moment* was published in 1981. Sayers bridged literature and theology while he bridged theology and science.[14] Loder's approach resonated with me, because I had been working on interdisciplinary teams in the Texas Medical Center since 1974, especially at Texas Children's Hospital, M. D. Anderson Hospital, and later at Houston Child Guidance Center. The creative process was our common currency.

Loder related the creative process to ultimate matters by talking about a "fourfold knowing event." The first kind of knowing is what we understand about our lived world, which we compose as a reality "out there," and which in turn composes us.[15] We also create relationships. From *being* in these relationships we sense that "being-itself" is revealed as "Holy." The "self cannot be itself unless it is grounded in the Source," as he said, which "lets it be."[16] The third part of the "knowing event" takes place when our two-dimensional world, where we usually live and relate to others, is "violated" by the void.

To speak of "nothing," Loder cautioned us, is "a semantic anomaly," because it allows us to speak of nothing as if it were something.[17] Still, he pressed on to talk about the void as the negation of the first two kinds of knowing. The fourth dimension of this knowing event is when the Holy moves from the background behind the void into the foreground and replaces it, as one's primary existential reference. This is the "transforming moment."

Loder stressed the immediacy of this event and wrote that the graciousness of being-itself comes out of nowhere and mediates between God and humanity.[18] He called such events "convictional experiences," because they are decisive and self-authenticating although it seems to me that it is difficult if not impossible for any event to be "self-authenticating." There is always a context and a history to consider, as in all the personal experiences Loder used to illustrate the transforming moment from his own life and his counseling experience with others. He was already involved in the Christian milieu of his family and was reading Christian theology when his earlier experiences took place. He was a professor at Princeton when his major transforming experience took place. His counseling sessions were also primarily with seminary students. Considering the context and history for these experiences does not undermine Loder's argument so much as it makes the case for the importance of an early absorption and activation of classical Christian language to help make sense of and evaluate such encounters.

Loder's great contribution was to apply the ordinary use of the creative process, which we are all aware of, to the existential setting. The conflict that sets the process in motion is when the two-dimensional experience of the world is shattered by the experience of the void. The insight that resolves this conflict is when the Holy gives ultimate meaning to the three-dimensional experience. As he said, "in ordinary experience transformation begins and ends with the development of the personality's creative and adaptational capacities." In "the theological context" the pattern begins with "Christ's initiative" which brings one through the experience of the void into faith to guide one's daily life and worship.[19]

As already mentioned, I experienced the void as a child. Later, as a mountain climber, I often felt its vertigo while being exposed to vast expanses of emptiness. I fell into the void twice, once in the Rockies and once in the Alps. The experience of being in the void, however, left no trace. The falling began with the faint scrape of a boot slipping across tiny rock crystals or twisting out of a hold, but consciousness did not return until I was hanging upside down at the end of a rope, getting oriented to climb out of danger. This is why Godly Play talks more about "limits" and "boundaries" than the experience of the void, as if it were something we could know. Either way, as Gabriel Marcel has reminded us, there is no "tower" one can climb up to look out over the existential boundary to see what is on "the other side." There is only the boundary we cannot know beyond whether we talk of limits or the void.

A brief reminder needs to be inserted here. In conversations with Buddhists the terms *emptiness* or *void* are not negative. They do not point to meaninglessness, a lack of truth and reality, or nothingness, but to a way of life. To a Buddhist "the void" denotes a certain fullness of wisdom. It is a goal to be sought, not avoided. What is at work here, however, in both East and West, is to discover a way to cope with our existential anxiety, not just the experience of personal emptiness but the ultimate and nonspecific threat of our limits.

The first step to cope with our existential anxiety is to note what Gabriel Marcel, Dorothy Sayers, and others have warned us about. Existential mysteries, such as our limits to being and knowing, cannot be completely solved without remainder like a problem, whether in simple mathematics or in a detective story, because they involve the totality of our being. We can talk in general about our limits, as we are doing now, but to know them personally we need to participate in them and that leaves us speechless. To engage the ultimate environment the self must become permeable to allow the mystery to seep into us to be known.[20]

What is *beyond* the limits to being and knowing makes us existentially anxious, because we don't know exactly what to fear. Godly Play helps children cope with this non-specific danger by inviting them to enter classical Christian language, such as the parable of the Good Shepherd, with their senses, reason, and contemplation. Since the nonspecific danger is to the whole being, the whole person needs a way to respond with awareness without being overwhelmed.

Loder's four-fold act of knowing influenced Godly Play in general, but the more specific influence comes from Irving Yalom's *Existential Psychotherapy*. Yolam is now a professor emeritus of psychiatry at Stanford University School of

Medicine. The four existential limits he encountered most in his clinical practice were death, the need for meaning, the threat of freedom, and aloneness.[21] Such issues do not yield to therapy. They are realities one must cope with. They define us, so they need to be brought within our awareness as part of our authentic being. If we do not do this, the energy that could be used for living and healing is drained away. It is wasted to shore up the walls of repression, constructed to prevent consciousness of the limits that help define our true nature.

The repression of our existential limits is a major reason why adults maintain the fiction that children are always happy. Adults hope this is so, but that is cheap hope. It masks adult limits we share with children, and it hides from the responsibility to listen respectfully when children try to tell us about their ultimate concerns. This neglect traps children in a double bind. They must either please the adults and repress their anxiety or express their anxiety and risk having adults ignore, dismiss, and shame them. This is why children usually remain silent about their ultimate concerns, which ironically seems to confirm that they are always happy.

The play therapists at Texas Children's Hospital, especially Jackie Vogel, in the mid-1970s were the first to understand Godly Play and what "the chaplain's strange language" had to do with children's ultimate concerns, which are obvious in a hospital setting. The play therapists knew quite well how to help children cope with the fear of the unknown. They could help children play this out, for example, with a model of the hospital's surgical suite to make going there more familiar and to help the children talk about their fears. However, when children asked, "Am I going to die?" something changed in the communication. This was not a question about the unknown. This was about the unknowable, so a whole different kind of language was necessary. The parable of the Good Shepherd needed to replace the model of the surgical suite to make the existential meaning required to adequately respond to such a question.

Children know about this shift in communication. They are aware that talking about death is different, so they don't ask about death so much as dying. Will it hurt? Will you stay by me? Will you help me? Life at the edge is leveling. It is hard to tell who is a child and who is an adult. Children know that death is personal and that they are a case of one. They are not distracted by statistics. This is why it is good to meet children as a storyteller rather than an expert about religion. The parable of the Good Shepherd[22] is told, not explained. It is placed between you and the child so the two of you can enter the middle realm in the story to be with God and mutually bless each other as meaning is created.

The sheep are brought out from the safety of the sheepfold and are moved through the grass, by the water, and through places of danger back to the sheepfold. The wolf approaches and ordinary people run away, but in the parable the wolf can also be touched. Should it be buried? Pushed away? Should it come into the sheepfold? Will it change? How can the Good Shepherd stand between you and the wolf? He gives his life for the sheep? Amazing. *Telling* the story and *moving* the pieces of the parable is the kind of "thinking" that needs to be done by the whole child and shown how to do by the whole mentor. Entering the parable to create existential meaning with the Creator has a pattern to it, which is very important for understanding Godly Play's development and the process of how to be with children in the middle realm.

The Pattern of the Creative Process

The literature about the creative process has changed enormously since Loder first described the structure of the transformational process as "the Hypnagogic Paradigm" in 1966.[23] This was forty years after Graham Wallas published *The Art of Thought* with its four steps for the creative process—preparation, incubation, illumination, and verification—and forty-six years before R. Keith Sawyer's second edition of *Explaining Creativity: The Science of Innovation*. Sawyer included a comprehensive history of the concept's interpretation as well as an up to date analysis of its many dimensions.[24]

Still, within this almost ninety-year span there is still much to learn from Sayers and Loder. Their two descriptions of the pattern of the creative process may be compared as follows:

Sayers	Loder/Godly Play
	1. Opening the process
	2. Scanning
1. The Idea (Insight)	3. Insight
2. Incarnation in an Appropriate Form	4. Development
3. Communication	5. Closure/Communication

Sayers did not speculate on where "The Idea" comes from for the human maker, but modern research has been very interested in this. Still, as this summary shows, the pattern of the two views is similar and continues to show how the human process is analogous to the Creator's nature as described in the creeds.

Loder originally placed the origin of the creative process in the state of consciousness between sleep and wakefulness,[25] an in-between state like the middle realm. This connotation was later lost when Loder began to speak more abstractly about "the transformational process"[26] and "transformational logic,"[27] although in his teaching he remained very personal and direct in his communication about his own experiences of transformation.

Descriptions of the creative process in Godly Play have likewise evolved. In *Godly Play* and *Teaching Godly Play* the description turns around the circle of how the process feels, but in *Children and the Theologians*[28] the four dimensions of the creative process are pictured in parallel to show how flow, play, love, and contemplation are similar in structure so they are likely to have come from the same source. Where Loder and Godly Play differ will be noted in the following overview of the creative process's five steps.

1. Opening

The process begins with a conflict, as Loder suggested, but there are hard openings and soft ones. A hard opening usually involves a dramatic loss such as the death of a loved one, or a doctor's diagnosis of cancer, that shatters one's assumed world. Soft openings, on the other hand, result from encountering some richness in life that dissolves one's ordinary worldview. Examples are a beautiful sunset, tiny tundra flowers above the timberline, and the ocean's placid calm or wild fury. Such events, or the art that evokes them, cause one to wonder. Positive wonder can stimulate scanning as much as a negative crisis.

Loder used examples from his own life and from his counseling sessions, which were usually hard openings, but he also provided a few examples of soft openings such as when Bulgakov, the great Russian Orthodox theologian, was "driving across the southern steppes of Russia" or when he encountered

Raphael's Sistine Madonna in a Dresden art gallery.[29] Most spiritual guidance with children on a regular basis involves soft openings, which is why Godly Play emphasizes wonder, beauty, and play in its method. Mentors, however, are always ready to provide care and support for hard openings, such as in the hospital when a child's assumed world is shattered by treatment or in the parish when a divorce threatens to fragment a child's sense of world coherence.

2. Scanning

The second step for both Loder and Godly Play is scanning. Loder counseled that the search can be brief, only a few minutes, or much longer, such as my ten-year search for a method (1960 to 1970) to enlarge the capacity of Christian education. The scanning process moves relentlessly toward a new and more adequate meaning once it begins, as Dorothy Sayers also recognized. When a more adequate vision is intuited, it forces its way into consciousness as an insight, like when Thea and I were watching our girls in the Montessori school and discovered the key to rethinking Christian education. Insight, however, is not inevitable. Frustrations such as rigidity and repression can block the process and it can be used in destructive ways. We will return to this in a moment.

3. Insight

Insight can be correlated to a burst of brain activity. There is "a spike of gamma-wave rhythm," which is the highest electrical frequency generated by the brain.[30] The moment of insight can also be predicted by a steady rhythm of alpha waves emanating from the right hemisphere about eight seconds before the insight takes place.[31] What this confirms is that we are not "imagining" things when we sense that the creative process is at work or that an insight is about to happen. This scientific description, however, only provides a correlation between the biological phenomenon described and one's awareness of the process's movement. Shifting to the domain of scientific language does not necessarily demonstrate a cause.

Loder divided the insight into two parts, the insight itself and another step, which is a sense of moving forward. Godly Play combines these two aspects within the insight, because they occur almost simultaneously and because more emphasis is given by Godly Play than Loder to the next two steps, which are development and closure.

4. Development

The whole creative process is optimally channeled through one's special interests and capacities, but it is especially in development that this becomes evident. In Godly Play these alternative pathways are recognized and the description of Howard Gardner is used to give this awareness specificity. Gardner's view of multiple intelligences (MI) contradicts the idea that human beings have a single, general intelligence. This idea was first presented in 1983 and in 2011 Gardner looked back over the development of his idea in the latest edition of *Frames of Mind: The Theory of Multiple Intelligences*. He wrote, "I am sticking to my 8½ intelligences, but I can readily foresee a time when the list could grow, or when the boundaries among the intelligences might be reconfigured."[32] The frames of knowing he presently recognizes are: linguistic, musical, logical-mathematical, spatial, bodily-kinesthetic, interpersonal, intrapersonal, and naturalistic. The one-half frame is an existential one, which is when children and adults are drawn toward ultimate things. As the frames of knowing developed he included spirituality and moral sensitivity within each of the other frames, but he has, at last, acknowledged that there are people with a special interest and sensitivity to matters of ultimate concern. Mentors in Godly Play rooms with children have known for decades that this ultimate interest can be manifest quite early in child development.

Gardner specifically related his theory of multiple intelligences to creativity in 1993. His *Creating Minds: An Anatomy of Creativity*[33] illustrated the types of creativity by using examples. A creative insight might be developed in intra-psychic terms like Freud, in mathematical terms like Einstein, in visual art like Picasso, in music like Stravinsky, in words like T. S. Eliot, in dance like Martha Graham, or in social terms like Gandhi. Godly Play mentors are attuned to the many ways that children prefer to make meaning so they can support the optimum development of their insights.

Questions have been raised about whether Gardner's criteria for defining his frames are adequate. A second query is whether all of his "intelligences" are really needed to adapt to life's demands. For example, couldn't dance and music be "talents"? Third, is there sufficient empirical evidence to support his conceptualization? Despite these important queries, the use of this theory in education for about thirty years has established it and Godly Play makes use of it.

5. Closure

Loder's last step is verification, but in Godly Play that is part of the development step. Perhaps, this was because Loder was describing the overwhelming presence of Christ, which was considered "convictional" or self-authenticating. He may have assumed that the process virtually closes on its own in such a case, however in other situations closure can even be *forced against* one's will by internal or social pressures or both.

Closure involves the creator's decision-making style and will-to-close, as well as the need to balance the lure of perfection against what is good enough to carry one's new idea forward to completion and communication.

The closure of this process might be hard or soft, as with the opening. A hard closure is rigid and is focused on the idea alone. It is difficult to open again. A soft closure, on the other hand, is firm but not rigid. It is focused on the creative process as a whole and as integrated with the person. It is not isolated as something we do but remains connected to who we are.

The Use and Misuse of the Creative Process

There is nothing in the pattern of the creative process that guarantees constructive outcomes. As Winnicott said, transitional space is the place where creativity, play, art, and religion come from, but it can also be corrupted as the source for stealing, lying, fetishism, obsessive rituals, and other destructive practices. What matters is whether its use is integrated with the integrated flow, play, love, and contemplation that is at our core as creative beings, as will be discussed in the next chapter.

An example of the misuse of the creative process is to be a clever thief. Creative theft might be white-collar crime as well as other kinds. An action-based example was studied by Ikuya Sato. He reported in "Bosozoku: Flow in Japanese Motorcycle Gangs" that the thieves he studied exhibited all the personal satisfaction of creative flow, but the outcome was still anti-social and destructive.[34]

The misuse of the creative process for lying has also been studied. Dan Ariely at Duke University examined this in *The (Honest) Truth About Dishonesty*.[35] It takes creativity to lie to others, but the more destructive use of the creative process is to first deceive yourself to have the confidence to deceive others well. This uses the creative process to attack the fundamental core of who we are meant to be. It usually takes the form of thinking that we are more intelligent and popular than we are. This creates the illusion that we are too clever, too well-liked, or too important to get caught.

Another misuse has to do with the rigidity of the closure of the process, when it becomes detached from the creative flow, play, love, and contemplation of our core. Loder noted that sometimes "people who have undergone remarkable experiences of transformation become authoritarian about scripture and spiritual laws." He wondered what caused the incongruity between "the freeing transformation and the rigid aftermath" and proposed three causes.[36]

The first cause of rigidity is fear. The "awesomeness of the Holy" results in "the suspicion that one is not quite oneself afterward" and people begin to worry about "losing the good thing that has happened." The fear of losing control and of losing "the good thing" can combine with the "fear of aspersions cast on the experience by other people" to produce "an aggressive, authoritarian posture to defend the authenticity of the Holy and to drive away all detractors."

The second cause of rigidity comes from confusing God's power with personal power. When the dramatic experience of "the Spirit begins to wane, one tries to keep it or retrieve it, resulting in the temptation to substitute personal power for the Power of God." The resulting arrogance, *even if unconscious and not intended*, is blasphemy, a lack of reverence for God and contempt for the Holy.

The third cause of rigidity is a "general lack of thoughtful language about God's Spirit." People who experience God's presence desire to speak about it, but they are not always well equipped. As Loder put it, "One wants to say more but, not knowing how, says the same cliché three times, with ever-increasing volume." The "general lack of thoughtful language" does not necessarily indicate a lack of biblical language, which may be parroted, in ways disconnected with our constructive, creative core. Sometimes religious language is even used to attack other people and even one's own well being.

In the Godly Play room the children are surrounded by stories about people who have come so close to God and God has come so close to them that they know what God wants them to do. Moses, Abraham, and Mary are examples of people who have struggled to do what is right and to speak the truth. They have also been recreated by God's presence to become graceful people who generously do the right thing and speak the truth by nature. In an open classroom there is ample opportunity to build this kind of behavior into the life of the community.

Since these biblical stories are not declaimed, proclaimed, or announced in an overly solemn or authoritarian way and since rigid and authoritarian behavior is not modeled in the Godly Play room, it is also unlikely that the practice of Godly Play will result in rigidity. Instead, children are invited into the experience of knowing the Creator with their own creative core in the middle realm. Rather than stealing, lying, and rigidity, Godly Play fosters the art of playful orthodoxy to promote creating constructive ideas, including one's own newness of life, that are deeply connected to original grace.

Christian Language and the Wholeness of the Creative Process

The creative process has two phases, opening and closing. There is a danger of getting stuck in either. The "liberal" part of the process is related to the opening and the "conservative" orientation is related to the closing. Supporting the use of the whole process while learning Christian language helps prevent irrationally separating the two tendencies into two ways of life or political positions within or outside the church.

Each of the five steps in the creative process also has a type of person who is especially drawn to it. There are openers, scanners, discoverers, developers, and closers. You may have served on adult committees where all five types were represented and you can see all five types among the children moving about in the Godly Play environment. One of the many benefits of an open classroom is that mentors who are sensitive to the steps in the creative process can guide children who are stuck in a particular step toward enjoying the whole circle of the creative process and, thus, help reintegrate their fundamental core.

When hard or soft openings are experienced some people are eager to proceed. These are the openers. Their opposite, the naysayers, however, will not budge. They sit by the doorway to the creative process with their arms folded, challenging anyone to arouse wonder or openness in *them*! Both openers and naysayers can get stuck in the first step of the process. Scanners, however, love to open and continue on to scan, but they are not very interested in discovering any particular insight, which might require taking responsibility for it. The third group, the discovers, are willing to be open and tolerate the anxiety caused by the chaos of scanning, because they enjoy the thrill of the insight. Once the insight is discovered, however, this kind of person often loses interest and does not always follow through to develop the idea. Developers do not like the chaos of opening, scanning, or the thrill of the insight, so they are likely to take over another's insight and develop it. Finally, the closer can't stand any of the preceding four steps.

She or he likes to stand back and decide which ideas, developed by other people, to keep and which to throw away. We need all five kinds of people. They all play a role, especially on teams for joint projects, but people who can move all the way through the whole process from opening to closure find a satisfaction that comes from exercising their fundamental wholeness, which contributes to their spiritual maturity.

Children in a Godly Play room who say things like "Oh, we had that already," are encouraged to move towards openness. Parables are especially useful for this. The scanners, who may wander aimlessly about in the open space, are supported to get out some specific material to make their own discoveries and to develop them. Children who love insights are especially encouraged to develop their discoveries and bring them to fruition. Children who copy other children's work to develop it are invited to use their own creative process to make personal meaning. Children who stand off to the side and make comments about other children's work are encouraged to move through the whole process from beginning to end so they can experience evaluating *their own work*. When mentors guide and support children through the whole process, children tend to find more satisfaction in completing the whole circle than living with the fractured grace of being stuck in one of the steps. Such wholeness is self-supporting and contributes to the child's continuing development. It liberates them from cultural constraints and inner limitations to be truly free to develop towards spiritual maturity.

In 1966 at the end of his *Religious Pathology and Christian Faith* Loder challenged us across the decades in a way that still rings true. "Christian education is structuring the creative act for the purpose of expanding the boundaries of freedom. Without this central emphasis, it becomes fantastic, and in

Kierkegaard's words: 'Christian education is a lie.'"[37] Godly Play has done its best to be truthful.

Conclusion

We began this chapter with a question: How *does* Godly Play feel? It feels like the middle realm out of which comes the creative process turning around its circle of opening, scanning, insight, development, and closure, but there is more. We are psychological, social, biological, and spiritual creatures, so the creative process is at work in each of these dimensions, seeking to bring deep unity back to our lives to recreate us. This is because the creative process is not merely something we use to create ideas. It is who we are as Christians, created in the image of God. To discuss this further and to connect the middle realm of Godly Play to life-long learning, we turn now to the next chapter.

5.

The Center-point
and Spiritual Maturity

When "things fall apart" will the center hold? William
Butler Yeats (1865–1939) asked this question and
longed for a second coming to renew the fundamental power
of a center-point:

> Turning and turning in the widening gyre
> The falcon cannot hear the falconer;
> Things fall apart; the centre cannot hold;
> Mere anarchy is loosed upon the world,
> The blood-dimmed tide is loosed, and everywhere
> The ceremony of innocence is drowned;
> The best lack all conviction, while the worst
> Are full of passionate intensity.
>
> . . . .
>
> And what rough beast, its hour come round at last,
> Slouches towards Bethlehem to be born?[1]

Original grace strains with primal intensity to be renewed in a world where "the ceremony of innocence is drowned." Children need good guides to help them identify this original grace and to give it expression in classical Christian language, which in turn supports the community of the church to help guide them toward becoming non-naïve and consciously graceful adults.

This chapter joins the continuing consideration of the creative process with reflections on developmental psychology to explore how one moves from being a child to becoming like a child to be spiritually mature as a graceful person. The creative process is not just how we create ideas. It is also who we are and can provide a center that does hold.

The Center that Holds: The Four Dimensions of the Creative Process

We are creatures with biological, psychological, social, and spiritual dimensions, so the center we were born with, our original grace, can also be expected to become complex. Dylan Thomas caught this entwined complexity in the obliqueness of his poem, "The Force that through the Green Fuse Drives the Flower."

"Complexity," as we use it here, is not the opposite of simplicity, because it is more than intricacy, which suggests something that is only involved or perplexing. Complexity is the property of being closely connected and yet distinct. The creative process at our core begins in unity and then develops into four dimensions as the child grows and develops the language to help make such distinctions. Yeats experienced the return of this unified energy just before his death. He wrote in a letter:

I am happy and I think full of an energy I had despaired of. It seems to me that I have found what I wanted. When I try to put all into a phrase I say "Man can embody truth but he cannot know it." I must embody it in the completion of my life. The abstract is not life and everywhere drags out its contradictions. You can refute Hegel but not the Saint or the Song of Sixpence.[2]

The return to original grace, despite original sin, is a potential that is always available through alignment with the Creator and can result in graceful moments as one matures. More importantly, however, one can fulfill the original promise by living lasting, graceful lives. It is this kind of spiritual maturity that Jesus pointed to when he spoke about "becoming like a child" to enter his realm. This is also what T. S. Eliot pointed to near the end of "Little Gidding," the last of his *Four Quartets*:

> We shall not cease from exploration
> And the end of all our exploring
> Will be to arrive where we started
> And know the place for the first time.
>
> . . . .
>
> At the source of the longest river
> The voice of the hidden waterfall
> And the children in the apple-tree
> Not known, because not looked for
> But heard, half-heard, in the stillness
> Between two waves of the sea.
> Quick now, here, now always—
> A condition of complete simplicity

(Costing not less than everything)
And all shall be well and
All manner of thing shall be well
When the tongues of flame are in-folded
Into the crowned knot of fire
And the fire and the rose are one.[3]

To say more about our core complexity, let's borrow a strategy from comparative biology called "homology." This is the study of similar traits in different animals. The similarity in the differentness suggests a common ancestor. For example, if a particular bone is noticed in the forearm of a human, the leg of a dog, the wing of a bird, and the flipper of a whale, a single source is suggested.

The psychological, social, biological, and spiritual dimensions of the creative process share the same characteristics and structure, so, a common origin is suggested in the middle realm. Let's examine each of these four dimensions to see more clearly what these characteristics are like.

The Psychological Dimension of the Creative Process: "Flow"

The psychological study of the creative process took a leap forward in 1975 when one of the modern pioneers, Mihaly Csikszentmihalyi, published *Beyond Boredom and Anxiety*.[4] He argued that creativity appears in a middle range of activity between the extremes of tedious rigidity and anxiety-producing chaos. He found that this was true of many, seemingly diverse, activities, such as painting and mountain climbing, which he investigated. When one is overwhelmed by chaos or under-whelmed by boredom, creativity is frustrated. The middle way between chaos and rigidity is where creativity flourishes.

Csikszentmihalyi used the term "flow" to describe how the creative process feels when it is working smoothly. In 1990 he published a book that focused on flow's structure as the optimal experience.[5]

Flow involves many characteristics that are shared with play, love, and contemplation. First, there is deep concentration. The sense of self disappears. Time is altered and the experience is enjoyed for itself rather than for any product that might arise out of it. When feedback is relatively immediate and the goals are clear, then flow is sustained. One's skills need to be challenged but not overwhelmed.

The placing of creativity in a middle realm between being overwhelmed and under-whelmed is different from but does not exclude Loder's overwhelming "transforming moment" in an encounter with the void. Such a conflict stimulates the creative process to create *existential* meaning.[6]

There appears to be a kind of rhythm between drama and continuity that finds its way into many religions in many centuries. Harvey Whitehouse, who works in the overlapping fields of archeology, history, and psychology, proposed a theory about this.[7] He called the two tendencies toward drama and continuity "imagistic" and "doctrinal." Each is related to a specific kind of cognition, the "episodic memory system" for drama and the "semantic memory system" for continuity. Both are needed because continuity needs dramatic punctuation to keep the consistency alive and the consistency is needed to provide a safe context for the drama.

Csikszentmihalyi's focus on optimum experience led him to argue that flow is the key to the good life and is sustained by intrinsic motivation.[8] His scientific description of optimal experience, therefore, is a good companion for the theological study of the graceful person. The role of Godly Play in this conversation is to help children dwell in the middle realm as they absorb and activate classical Christian language through the flow of the creative process, which links this language system to the dynamic source of the Creator.

The benefit of flow can also be seen by studying what happens when flow is missing. Csikszentmihalyi did this in *The Evolving Self* and concluded that people will always seek the happiness associated with flow, even when they lack the discipline and knowledge to achieve it. They wind up settling for fake flow. He wrote that "in such cases, the result of seeking enjoyment is entropy, rather than harmony."[9] In other words, flow cannot be maintained by artificial means, such as by drugs, because the real and constructive challenges for true creativity are missing. Godly Play seeks to stimulate and support the reality of flow and to support its close relationship to play, love, and contemplation to help keep the potential alive for the reunification of the four dimensions of the creative process in the spiritual maturity of the graceful person.

The Social Dimension of the Creative Process: Play

There is a great deal of overlap between flow and play. In fact Csikszentmihalyi thought at first he was studying play before he carefully distinguished it from the creative process. As his project became clearer, he energized other students of creativity. Howard Gardner noted in his *Creating Minds* that when Csikszentmihalyi asked him, "Where is creativity?" instead of the usual, "What is creativity?" the scope of his study changed and took on new life.[10] Three years later Mihaly Csikszentmihalyi published the next step in his life-long study of creativity, which affirmed that creating is about two-thirds social.[11] In 2012 Jonah Lehrer's *Imagine: How Creativity Works*, a popular review of the field, was divided into two major sections: "Alone" (139 pages) and "Together" (114 pages). His presentation balanced the importance of the social and the solitary aspects of creativity and emphasized the importance of the right mixture of people for the social aspect of creativity to work well.[12]

The social aspect of creativity is something we all sense but don't always want to admit. A treasured idea may be personally new but not new in the history of Western Civilization! The step from personal to social originality is a big one, which involves skills, characteristics, and an environment that is favorable for the development of a new idea in addition to merely thinking up something original. Still, having ideas that are new personally is important and should be treasured.

Creativity may be both individual and social, but play is always social, even when it appears to be solitary. Take a climber alone on a mountain wall. The creative moves are made *with* the mountain and changing weather. The mountain's challenge is personal and existential, a matter of life and death. A less dramatic example is watching people play solitaire. They look alone, but the cards represent an imagined playmate to interact with.

Perhaps, the most radical view of play's social dimension was that of Johan Huizinga, the Dutch historian. In 1938 he played with the Latin title of his book *Homo Ludens*, to claim that human beings are essentially players. Play defines us more fundamentally than the ability to create and work with tools (*Homo Faber)* or the ability to use reason (*Homo Sapiens).* Huizinga's view of play has often been misunderstood. He was not talking about amusing ourselves, superficial silliness, or leisure activities. For him play was not an element *within* culture or an *alternative* to culture, both of which are interesting ideas.

He went much farther. Huizinga argued that play *is* culture, which is a truly challenging.

We will use Catherine Garvey's study of play to show how it is related to the creative process. Her study was first published in 1977 and claimed "play" to be indefinable, so she carefully listed five characteristics, instead of proposing a definition. The characteristics are that "play is pleasurable," "has no extrinsic goals," "is spontaneous and voluntary," and "involves some active engagement on the part of the player." The fifth quality included the social aspect of play. She wrote that "play has been linked with creativity, problem solving, language learning, the development of social roles, and a number of other cognitive and social phenomena."[13] In the enlarged edition of her book in 1990 she added two new chapters, both of which amplify the social dimensions of play. Garvey's five characteristics of play are similar to Csikszentmihalyi's description of flow's characteristics.[14]

The focus of Godly Play is on the community of children in the circle and what is *personally* new for them to affirm the flow of the creative process for each child and the wondering group. When children create something new, it is renewing and exciting for everyone. Encouraging such self-directed learning was part of the Montessori tradition from the beginning. To create meaning rather than being told answers arrived at by adults, personally integrates the meaning made with each child and stimulates the whole group. Since ultimate meaning is about one's personal life and death, it must be personally discovered to make a difference.

We have now seen the similarities between flow and play that involve both the characteristics of creating and the structure of the creative process. We turn now to the biological dimension of the creative process to continue examining this affinity.

The Biological Dimension of the Creative Process: Love

The biological dimension of the creative process is love. Like the other three dimensions of the creative process, love involves the whole person. After all, what could be more physical than "making love," which can result in the *creation* of new biological life? The attraction that draws people together is also very physical. A "limbic resonance" makes the match while the neocortex makes up reasons why the match is right.[15]

The limbic system is where our "emotional intelligence" resides. It is "a capacity that profoundly affects all other abilities either facilitating or interfering with them."[16] Since it developed before the neocortex, it can at times override our rationality.

The biological dimension of love is so deep in our origins that it has links to all our seven basic affect systems. The more cerebral nuances of feeling and thinking are blends, derived from these primary systems located in the old brain. Jaak Panksepp and Lucy Biven identified the seven systems as: *seeking*, *rage*, *fear*, *lust*, *care*, *panic/grief*, and *play*.[17]

Love is seeking. It moves toward newness, satisfaction, and creativity but is complicated by the rage associated with competing for scarce resources. Fundamental fear is not learned. It is a primal warning about danger during seeking. Lust is what pushes us toward creating offspring but is at times balanced with nonsexual caring for offspring and each other. Panic and grief come from the potential or actual loss of care and, finally, play is how we learn to manage the conflicts in the other affect systems, to give us the bio-psycho-social-spiritual blend we call love.

The kind of language most appropriate for connecting our thinking and emotions about love is poetry. It links the neocortex and the limbic system. In *A General Theory of Love*, the authors used an abridgement of Robert Frost's famous saying, "famous" at least among poets, to make their point. The saying was taken from a letter to Louis Untermeyer (January 1, 1916) and is: "A poem begins as a lump in the throat, a sense of wrong, a homesickness, a love sickness. It is never a thought to begin with."[18] This explains why the poetry of the Christian language system needs to be respected and celebrated. It helps connect the verbal and non-verbal aspects of love, so St. Paul's poem of love (1 Corinthians 13) will be used as our classical text to describe it.

Choosing Paul to describe love may sound odd when stressing the biological dimension of the creative process. Wasn't Paul against the body? This view of Paul may come from reading him through the lens of the third to the fifth centuries. Theologians such Origen, Evagrius, the Cappadocians, and Augustine contrasted the spiritual to the physical and used metaphors for the maturation of spirituality like climbing a ladder or a mountain toward God, which seemed to move one away from the physical. This view was heavily influenced by the Greek philosophy of Neoplatonism, but Paul's own view of the body was different.

Philip Sheldrake argued in *A Brief History of Spirituality* that what Paul meant by "the spiritual" was "life in the Spirit."[19] The Pauline letters contrasted "spirit" (*pneuma*) with "flesh" (*sarx*) as "two attitudes to life." If Paul had intended to contrast the spiritual and the "physical" he would have likely paired "spirit" (*pneuma*) with "body" (*soma*). This is why Sheldrake concluded that for Paul, "A 'spiritual person' (see 1 Corinthians 2:14–15) was simply someone within whom the Spirit of God dwelt or who lived under the influence of the Spirit of God."[20] There is nothing in his poem of love that negates the body.

Paul claimed that love is freely given and received. It is patient and kind. It is not jealous, not boastful, not arrogant, and not rude. Love is also deeply engaging. He wrote that it bears, believes, hopes, and endures all things. Love is so engaging that it lasts forever. Loving is done for itself. There is no extrinsic goal. That is why jealousy, arrogance, and boasting are not part of its reality. Language and people without love are empty, like "a noisy gong or a clanging symbol."

Love, also, has links to other kinds of activities, such as ethics and creating meaning, much like play does. In Paul's terminology love is connected to the spiritual gifts, which are nothing without love (1 Corinthians 12:27–13:2) and to ethics and physical action, where loving one's neighbor fulfils the law (Romans 13:10).

In addition love is pleasurable, but this pleasure is profound. It incorporates both the pain of the crucifixion and the longed for but perplexing wonder of the resurrection, a form of which Paul personally experienced on the road to Damascus when Jesus turned his life around. Love, therefore, includes the depth of pain and the height of happiness for the whole person. The mixture of pain and happiness produces joy, which is the realistic and quintessential Christian emotion.

When Paul contrasted God's Kingdom to the Roman Empire, he drew attention to a different kind of "place." It was a domain of righteousness, peace, and joy in the Holy Spirit (Romans 14:17). By contrast the Roman Empire was comprised of geography and the *Pax Romana* was kept in place by force of arms and taxes.

Paul's poem in the context of the collection of the letters ascribed to him provides a richly nuanced and expansive view of love with the characteristics and structure similar to and connected with the other three dimensions of the creative process.

This brings us to the fourth dimension of the creative process, which is spiritual.

The Spiritual Dimension of the Creative Process: Contemplation

John Cassian (c.360–435) learned about contemplation from the variety of contemplatives he visited in the desert of Egypt in the fourth century. He then traveled to Constantinople, where he was ordained deacon, and then to Rome. Finally, he settled in Gaul, near Marseilles, and in 415 built the Abbey of St. Victor, which shaped Christian monastic life for centuries to come. His work influenced Benedict's Rule in the sixth century and, thus, the later reforms of the Benedictine order by the Cistercians and Trappists. As we said in chapter four, a modern version of this tradition is still alive. Thomas Keating with others developed centering prayer, which is now widely used inside and outside the confines of the cloistered life.

Richard of St. Victor's definition of contemplation from the twelfth century will be the classic example we shall use. Richard, who was probably born in Scotland, traveled to Paris to study with the Augustinian canons, especially Hugh, at the Abbey of St. Victor. Richard became abbot from 1162 until he died in 1173 and was the primary spiritual writer in the West during the twelfth century. In the next century his work influenced Bonaventure (1221–1274), who was minister general of the Franciscan Order and taught at the University of Paris for a time when Thomas Aquinas was there. Bonaventure's *Itinerarium Mentis in Deum* (Journey of the Soul into God) is the main work that continued Richard's influence during the thirteenth century. In the next century Dante (1265–1321) wrote in his *Paradiso* that Richard of St. Victor was a person "who in contemplation was more than man."[21]

Richard was at home in the noisy disputations of the University of Paris and in the quiet of the cloister, so from personal experience he could distinguish the knowing of the body by the senses from the knowing of the mind by reason and the knowing of the spirit by contemplation. He also lived in a century when the traditions of romantic and divine love were still in conversation and "fed into the development of affective mysticism which in turn encouraged greater interest in the development of spiritual guidance."[22]

Richard's definition of contemplation was that "contemplation is the free more penetrating gaze of a mind suspended with wonder concerning the manifestations of wisdom."[23] Contemplation sets all distractions aside by the openness of wonder to be with God without words. This definition of contemplation shares the same basic characteristics and structure as the other three dimensions of the creative process.

In addition to the overlapping characteristics all four dimensions share the same structure. *The opening* is connected to the giftedness and voluntary aspect of the four dimensions. You cannot force someone to love, enjoy flow, play, or contemplate. *Scanning* is linked to the deep engagement and searching quality in all four dimensions. *Insight* is associated with engaging this process for itself without much thought of any product that might result. Insights appear, seemingly of their own volition, rather than being forced. *Development* connects flow, play, love, and contemplation to other parts of life. *Closure* brings satisfaction and enables the discovery to be communicated.

There are some differences among the characteristics of the four dimensions, but these are matters of detail and are held together by the same structure. They do not contradict but enrich each other. For example the details from Csikszentmihalyi's description of flow fill in, rather than conflict with the ways that love, play, and contemplation are discussed. Csik-szentmihalyi and Garvey have both added helpful nuances to Richard's "more penetrating gaze of a mind" and "suspension with wonder." They also help extend the meaning of his "manifestations of wisdom." The shared structures, therefore, help interpret and enrich *each other* as well as give definition to the creative process from which they come.

When our original unity falls apart the four dimensions of the creative process appear. When the four dimensions are reunited we become a person who not only creates new ideas but is someone whose life flows, plays, loves, and contemplates with the Divine. Our original grace is renewed in a non-naive and conscious way as a graceful person.

The falling apart of our original unity is necessary and unavoidable, but it does not completely define us. It is by this means that we become creators in the image and likeness of the Creator. As long as we drift in the dreaming innocence of Eden we can only be merged with God.

Unfortunately the language that fractured our original unity can also construct artificial walls, ceilings, and tangles to block our pilgrimage to maturity as Christians. These impediments block our community, which robs us of companions for the journey. Christian language acknowledges this but also keeps the possibility of renewal fresh and full of dynamic potential to guide us forward to where, as Eliot said, we arrive where we started from and yet know in a new way, as if for the first time.

Ceilings are self-imposed by miscommunication with ourselves and with God. Walls are constructed by miscommunication with each other and God. This means we need to open our toolbox once more. We have already taken out the tools of classical Christian language—sacred stories, parables, liturgical action, and contemplative silence—to absorb and activate them for the spiritual quest. We also took out the container for the middle realm in which Christian language needs to be absorbed and activated. It is now time to take out a third tool—the language trap detector. It alerts us to the misuse of faith, which can ossify and form ceilings and walls that block the spiritual quest.

Ceilings, Walls, Tangles, and the Misuse of Faith

In St. Paul's love poem he ended by saying that giving up childish ways, as adults, involved ending the effort to understand God by looking in a mirror. We need to look through the mirror to know God face to face. The same could be said about our relationships with other people, our deep self, and the natural world around us. Meeting face to face allows us to know by being known. This is why faith, hope, and love all need to abide in us, but especially love (1 Corinthians 12–13). It is love that grounds hope in reality and prevents it from becoming fantasy. Love and hope join with faith to keep it dynamic rather than degrading into a locked box that can imprison us. Love links the theological virtues—faith, hope, and love—with who we are as creators and how we know our Creator.

Gabriel Marcel confirmed this as an existentialist philosopher. He was also a Roman Catholic, a playwright, a musician, and, as an aside, someone who understood the work of Maria Montessori and what her schools were trying to do for children.[24] Marcel's *Creative Fidelity* was published in French during World War II, but it was not translated into English until 1964. My introduction to this book and Marcel's other writings took place in a seminar with Sam Keen at Princeton Theological Seminary, where I met Marcel personally in 1961. His influence permeated Godly Play from the beginning, because he did not think of faith in a narrow and static way as belief and security.

Marcel considered "faith" as "creative fidelity." Its experience integrates the creative process with the necessary commitments we must make to have an identity. This looks like a circle from a logical point of view, but the necessary commitments to create a self cannot be made without knowing oneself, and knowing oneself cannot be accomplished without commitments.

This "vicious circle," however, is only in "the mind of the bystander who views another's fidelity from the outside."[25] When one views fidelity from within, the experience feels like growth. Viewing fidelity from within, however, is not as simple as it may sound. Creative fidelity is obscured when I become "a spectator to myself."[26]

In Godly Play the emphasis is on the integration of the creative process's four dimensions and recognizing its continuation across the decades of adulthood, which requires soft closures to promote the maturity of creative fidelity. This is why we need to think carefully about faith. It is a secure place to venture out from, but it can also ossify and become a prison that blocks the pilgrim's progress.

Any study of faith (or hope or love) that makes one "a spectator" will fail. This is why we need to "tell all the truth but tell it slant," as Emily Dickinson might say, so that faith's reality will "dazzle gradually" to avoid causing blindness. Marcel used phenomenology to do this. He bracketed his preconceptions and thinking about faith to experience it as directly as possible and then described the experience in a stream of consciousness in his journals. Unfortunately this approach renders one almost unable or unwilling to speak, preferring to dwell in faith, hope, and love than to talk about such experiences.

Godly Play invites children into the middle realm to experience the theological virtues, which as Thomas Aquinas said in Question 62, Articles 1–4 of the *Summa Theologia*, gives us much happiness. Love draws faith and hope into the absorbing and activating of Christian language, so the theological virtues saturate the words and creative process used to make existential meaning. This is why Christian language and the community it ties together is so valuable to identify the experience of God, express it, name it, and to provide the perspective to evaluate it. Unfortunately, this language, like faith itself, can become detached from its proper use to become an inert, objective entity rather than a dynamic tool.

Children need some sense of this danger, at least intuitively, as they build their foundations for lifelong learning. As the psalms say, God is a rock and fortress (Psalm 18:2) as well as a living spring (Psalm 36:9), so we need to be aware of the ceilings and walls that can be built by blocks of ossified faith, which can separate us from hope and love as well as the paradox of the Psalms.

The most useful trap detector I have found comes from an adaptation of the work of James W. Fowler, which he called "faith development." This term makes it unclear whether he was studying faith itself or how we communicate about faith. I have chosen the latter interpretation and used Fowler's work in Godly Play, not to understand how faith develops but to see how our communication about faith changes across the life span and how the language of faith can block the spiritual quest.

To study faith objectively, as an experience, distorts it, as Marcel argued, because faith includes love and hope[27] as well as creativity.[28] He argued that there is always a link between "I believe" and "I exist."[29] Still, Fowler and his associates took this risk and studied faith as sensitive onlookers. Even if his study could not escape distorting faith by the method he used to understand it, Fowler's work has helped Godly Play provide a way to think about communication with others and ourselves concerning ultimate matters, which has been an enormous help to keep the door open for life long learning.

When we leave behind the study of creativity and enter the world of developmental psychology, we enter a different academic space, which was one of the problems with the debate between Loder and Fowler in the 1980s. Developmental psychology and studies in creativity grew out of a common interest in "emergence" in the late nineteenth century, which was represented by such thinkers as Hegel, Darwin, and Comte. They all used some form of stages to understand the present by the steps it took to arrive there. Still, creativity studies and developmental psychology evolved different research traditions and vocabularies, which has made it very hard for scholars in these two areas to work together. Today, however, it has become increasingly apparent that the two fields belong together.[30] Godly Play, however, used Fowler's and Loder's models together from the 1970s, because creation applies both to new stages and new ideas. A related second reason was that we are fundamentally creators as human beings, so human development is the study of how we create ourselves as well as create new ideas.

My introduction to Fowler was in 1974 when I read his article "Toward a Development Perspective on Faith" in *Religious Education*. I flew to Boston at once and found myself sitting in his spacious office at Harvard Divinity School.

What struck me most, as we got acquainted, was his story about going on pastoral visits with his father, also a Methodist minister. He remembered listening and watching as his father talked to different people in different ways. What became known as "faith development" was conceived of as a way to make explicit what his father and other experienced clergy knew by intuition.

He also told me about working with the legendary Carlyle Marney from 1968 to 1969. Marney had created a safe and confidential environment he called Interpreter's House, where people could come to tell their stories to gain perspective on their lives. He gathered a cadre of sensitive, welcoming, and attuned listeners like Fowler, to help the visitors clarify their identity and values by storytelling. This experience confirmed for Fowler that he was on the right track. The name "Interpreter's House" came from John Bunyan's seventeenth-century classic *Pilgrim's Progress*. Fowler's personal journey became one to help the progress of other pilgrims by listening well.

My meeting with Fowler took place a little over a decade after meeting Gabriel Marcel, so my orientation to his work included Marcel's effort as a philosopher to use reason to understand the limitations of reason for talking about faith. His circle of creativity and certainty had already found its way into Godly Play, but Piaget's work, which heavily influenced Fowler's stages, also resonated with me. Piaget was being used widely to understand how children's thinking developed in the hospitals, schools, and churches where I was working in the 1970s. These three overlapping contexts—Fowler, Marcel, and Piaget—gave Godly Play a sound, practical flexibility for understanding and applying Fowler's theory to communicate with children and adults about spiritual growth and development.

Fowler's theory was useful for the evolution of Godly Play in at least four ways. First, it helped guide the creation of lessons and materials to avoid artificial ceilings and walls. The strategy used to prevent artificial structural limits was to work out the core metaphor for each sacred story, parable, or liturgical action and then trim away all extraneous language to leave the core image, expressed in very essential language, that was open to both children and adults. This did away with most of the structural distractions. The use of essential language *combined with the use of the materials* kept communication open to all the children in the circle and the adult mentors in the room.

Fowler's model was also used as a way to be aware of children as part of human development across the lifespan. Children were never disconnected from the adult journey toward spiritual maturity. Some developmental schemes don't take as large a view of human development as Fowler's. Freud's psychosexual stages, Montessori's "planes of development," and Piaget's "stages of cognitive development" ended with young adulthood. Even Kieran Egan's contemporary, "anti-stage" developmental scheme ends with ironic thinking, which appears during young adulthood. Fowler's vision, however, extends into old age, like the psycho-social model of his primary mentor, Erik Erikson.

Third, Fowler's model expanded Godly Play's thinking horizontally as well as in length across the lifespan. He used seven themes to determine a stage: cognitive development, perspective taking, the development of moral thinking, the relation to authority, the range of social reference, the form of world coherence, and finally how one thinks about the use of symbols.

Fowler's stages were based on 359 interviews. They were recorded and for the most part transcribed, so teams could check each other's interpretation and calculate the stages of the people interviewed to correlate the stages that emerged with age groups. The sample ranged from three and one-half to eighty-four years of age with an almost equal representation between males and females.[31]

There is much in Fowler's theory to be concerned about and much he also worried about, but to my knowledge none of his critics has carried out a project of equal magnitude to replicate his study and properly test it. The breadth of his stages has provided an eclectic richness of insight that includes most major ways of thinking about communication. This may be like mixing apples and oranges but Fowler's model still remains a state of the art collection of points of view for understanding how we communicate and think about ultimate matters.

A fourth use of Fowler's model, when abridged, is to have a handy and quick way to detect artificial ceilings and walls, so they can be worked through or worked around in the immediate moment. It is hard to use the whole model in the midst of children swirling around an open classroom or even sitting in the circle wondering, because there are forty-two cells to account for, but these stages are not hardwired into the brain. They are more like useful summaries of the kinds of thinking that people use at different times in their lives to guide their spirituality, so an abridgement provides a quick way to estimate where people are coming from to improve communication.

The reason this rule of thumb needs to be quick with its estimates of another person or group's preferences is because even a brief break in the communication to "stage someone" objectifies that person. Children are more sensitive to such pauses than adults, because they often read the person rather than listening to what they are saying. Communication is not aided by turning one's conversation partner into an object during the learning of Christian language, because this frustrates the mutual blessing of children and adults.

Despite all of these concerns and limitations, Fowler's model is still useful to guide one's intuition about the language preferences of children and adults as well as the multiple ways people communicate with themselves. For example we don't always think about religion in the same way on Sunday in worship as we do on Monday at work. How do we talk to ourselves about that? A detector for language walls, ceilings, and tangles is needed, but how would that work?

A Language-Trap Detector for the Spiritual Quest

We will reduce Fowler's seven themes for each stage to one, the "form of world coherence" to create a language-trap detector. This will enable us to be more alert about our perspective-taking when we sort out communication problems that can frustrate or even block the spiritual quest.

Perspective-taking is not just feelings or empathy. It is how people think others are thinking about them as they communicate. I remember walking out on a stage for a piano recital when I was about six. I got about halfway to the piano and stopped. As I looked out at all those people, I didn't realize they were also looking at me. While they were wondering why I didn't continue on to the piano and begin playing I was thinking about how amazing they all looked sitting there.

Perspective-taking develops from a lack of awareness that others are thinking about you, as when I was a child, to simple person-to-person patterns, to situations involving groups in which people are thinking about each other in a group while the group as a whole is thinking about you. Perspective taking cautions us to listen well to the ways that people express their sense of world coherence.

Ways of Thinking about World Coherence

The reduction of Fowler's theory to only one of its seven themes leaves behind the richness of his study, but it gives us a quick way to make a useful guess about coping with potential ceilings and walls. The preferences for considering how one's world fits together begins before language and ends after language, which is also a slight departure from Fowler's stages.

In Fowler's theory the stages are like walking up a flight of stairs. Each step is a stage. Today development is less stage-bound and is thought about more like an inclined ramp. A third view of change is that language preferences are like hopping around on a flat surface. My preference is the ramp image, which does not make sharp distinctions between stages, but still includes a logical progression in one's communication preferences.

We start up the ramp as infants and young children before language. It is then that we have an undifferentiated view of the world, which is fluid since it is not yet coded into the categories of language. The energy of God's undifferentiated presence, as in the mother's smile, is everywhere. This kind of world coherence is more important in Godly Play than in Fowler's work, because his study was dependent on spoken interviews. Godly Play, on the other hand, is equally concerned with the unspoken as well as the spoken lesson in teaching and learning.

As language develops young children begin to use it to give their world coherence and stability by reducing the flow of experience into episodes, like loosely held pearls in the palm of your hand. When children desire more coherence and stability than episodic thinking can give them, the episodes they previously used are strung together with a narrative, like stringing pearls into a necklace. Overarching stories are used by late childhood to collect individual stories into various meta-stories—such as those about the family, one's culture, and religious traditions. This is like a rope necklace made from several strands of pearls.

After a time, perhaps during adolescence, narrative is considered naïve, at least this has been true in the West since the eighteenth century. Concepts are considered the best way to hold one's world together. They are like tags replacing the actual pearls with descriptions and prices. We gain something and lose something each time we change preferences, but none of them disappear.

Young adults continue to accumulate training in special languages and experience with language in general. They become more flexible about considering their own thinking, so they notice that concepts change, compete, and overlap in their descriptions of the world's coherence. A new kind of narrative is needed to organize this complexity. A re-mythologizing takes place after de-mythologizing stories into concepts. A more complex narrative begins to be used to organize concepts into their own histories and into one's identity.

Finally, confidence in language begins to fade as the best means to communicate with God and each other about what really matters in life and death. Language itself—episodes, simple and complex narrative, concepts, and narratives about concepts—gives way to face-to-face communication with God, others, nature, and oneself, although knowing God face-to-face can take place at any time and in any form.

Fowler may have only found one person who met the characteristics he hoped to examine empirically for his proposed last stage. The only published interview of a person in the universalizing stage that I know of is a four-page excerpt in *Life Maps*,[32] a 1978 book about the interplay between faith and the emotional life, which involved Sam Keen, Jim Fowler, and myself. In his later publications Fowler used historical persons such as Gandhi, Martin Luther King, Jr., Thomas Merton, and others as examples.

Fowler's scheme appears to require people to have moved through all of the stages prior to universalizing before one begins to have doubts about language in general. This is in part true, but there is another way to look at this. Consider Mother Teresa. She was not interested in concepts, much less re-mythologizing. She was interested in people, so stories worked best for what she needed to know. Think also about Fred Rogers. Fred never stepped outside of narrative to talk about children by using concepts. In both cases the personal quality of communication was powerful, mindful, and mature.

Perhaps the interplay between spoken and unspoken communication can be explained by thinking in terms of foreground and background. In young children there is no language, so nonverbal communication is the only option. As the use of language begins to develop, the nonverbal is still in the foreground but language is now in the background. Around five to seven years of age children begin to read and write and attend school. Language now comes into the foreground and the nonverbal communication moves into the background. As one continues to develop the nonverbal usually stays in the background, but with people like Mother Teresa and Fred Rogers the nonverbal moves forward and can become more important than what is said. The nonverbal is harder to use as one moves beyond story because each person's personal space and time are left behind as one begins to think in abstractions. As one moves on beyond concepts to post-conceptual narrative as a preferred way of communicating there is still always the option to use narrative to convey one's meaning and personal connection, but it is never as simple as it once was when there was no alternative.

People with a lifetime of experience with the varieties of language structures become very effective listeners and guides. Godly Play mentors aspire to this awareness so they can avoid trapping children in low-ceilinged or narrow-walled traps that will block their spiritual quest. This is what makes having a rule of thumb to detect language ceilings, walls, and tangles so important.

A Rule of Thumb for Good Listening and Speaking

This rule of thumb to detect language ceilings, walls, and tangles is based on the inner logic of Fowler's stages. For example you need to mythologize (think in narrative) before you can de-mythologize and you can't re-mythologize unless you have de-mythologized. In short, you can't "move on" from structures found to be inadequate if you have never experienced them. Perhaps, the most obvious and important example is that you can't be childlike if you are still a child.

Adults sometimes long for the immediacy they left behind as children, but they forget that the fluid, magical thinking of children can be chaotic and sometimes terrifying. This is why older children and adults prefer the routine of their narrative and conceptual structures. Such stages appear to give us more control, even at the cost of lost vividness and immediacy. To become childlike is not as simple as it may seem. It is a "condition of simplicity" that costs "not less than everything," as T. S. Eliot said.

To guess another's communication preference you need to be aware of your own so you won't project it on your conversation partner. We usually think we are in the stage just beyond where they actually are. If you think you prefer concepts then you are likely at the complex story stage or in transition toward a preference for concepts. Being drawn "upward" happens because the stage "one up" is likely to appear better equipped to deal with problems experienced at one's current stage.

The stage just left behind is the one that most frustrates us, which makes sense since its limitations are still keenly felt. If you hate fundamentalists, you have probably just left behind a rigid story stage but are not yet at the concept stage. If you are still in transition, you don't have much perspective on your former preference except for the pain of its narrowness, as recently experienced.

The stage actually inhabited most of the time is somewhere in between the one admired and the one found most frustrating. Many people find themselves in a transition between story and concept, which feels like not wanting to rely too much on generalities even though we know they are built up from specific instances. Stories are still valued as personal and allowing for uniqueness, specific space, and a given time rather than dealing only with the abstract. We feel we are still a case of one, not a unit in a hypothetical construct.

This rule of thumb, despite its roughness, is enough to alert us to the fact that we communicate in different ways and our preference may not match that of our conversation partner. If I communicate with you in a way that is one stage above your preference, you may be drawn to it, as I said, but if I communicate in the style you just left behind, you are likely to find what I am saying to be hopelessly stupid and inadequate. How I talk may even make you angry. If I talk in a way that is two stages beyond where you are comfortable, then my ideas will be dismissed as over-intellectual and hopelessly out of touch. As an aside, this means that the final two stages Fowler described, here abridged as *re-mythologizing* and *beyond language*, are most likely to be thought of as absurd and childish by most people from a narrative perspective. This may be one of the reasons that talking about becoming like a child to enter God's realm has been so easily dismissed by the church.

Narrative feels most real to most people most of the time, regardless of age. That is why television commercials always begin with a story. It is good to be stretched toward concepts and the later kinds of thinking, but communicating one stage up *to teach that stage* is not the point. "Higher" is not better, because the point is to communicate in a way that builds community and understanding. This is a matter of common courtesy, which is the beginning of ethics.

In Godly Play it is important for mentors to know their own preferences, so they won't be tempted unconsciously to reframe how children think to match them. Children need to be around people who trust their way of thinking so they can go more deeply into its resources. One of the most tragic mistakes a mentor can make is to become angry with children when they talk in narrative, because one has left behind a rigid and narrow reliance on narrative as a preferred way of thinking. This is what the early Montessorians were talking about when they stressed the importance of humility for the teacher. Humility greatly helps good listening.

If children can absorb and begin to use Christian language in a way that is open to all the stages and styles of thinking about ultimate matters, then their journey and companions will not be limited at the beginning by artificial ceilings or walls or tied in knots by language tangles. This is why the whole toolbox that includes classical Christian language, the center-point of the middle realm, and the language trap detector is necessary for the spiritual quest.

Our original grace, the image of God, falls apart as we develop the ability to make distinctions by means of language and experience. This leads to a sense that the center does not hold, but when it is realized that the middle realm, as our center, is not static, or "fixity," as Eliot said, then its potential can be supported and encouraged as classical Christian language is absorbed and activated for the journey of a lifetime.

Lifelong learning, which helps us lean toward spiritual maturity, involves becoming like a child to renew our original grace despite the original sin of disintegration and broken communication. A good rule of thumb for listening and speaking to support and encourage life long learning is needed to help children build a good foundation in Christian language and yet remain open to the future. This is a future where the renewal of original grace can result in entering God's realm through the gateway of becoming like a child, where one can hear "children in the apple tree" and "hidden laughter."

Conclusion

The center that will hold is the creative process, which is not fixed but where the dance is, a dance with four dimensions—flow, play, love, and contemplation. This is the center-point that can with God's help recreate us in maturity as graceful people.

In the next and final chapter we will shift our perspective once again. We will discuss the diffusion and adaptation of Godly Play into the mainstream of Christian education. The paradox of keeping Godly Play's identity clear in the midst of diffusion and adaptation will then be examined. The pathways that spirituality might take into the future will be discussed in relation to Godly Play and at the very end a whimsical yet serious blessing will be given to see us all on our way.

6.

Spiritual Maturity
and Mutual Blessing

The language that flowed out of Christ's life, death, and resurrection becomes fully functional when it is absorbed and activated in the middle realm. This is what Godly Play tries to do, because this language that came from Christ is our way back to him and our way forward to becoming graceful people.

The middle realm is at the center of our relationship with ourselves, with others, with the earth, and with God. Centering on that point balances the flow of our personal creativity, the play of our social life with others, the linking of love's biology with that of the earth, and being utterly open spiritually to God through contemplation. This center-point gives us balance, like the still point of the spinning top. It is through the parables that our creativity is stimulated. The sacred stories give us identity through our social play. Liturgical action gives our biology meaning and through contemplative silence our creativity is joined with that of the Creator without the limitations of language.

The role of Godly Play in the mix of how Christianity is transferred from one generation to another is to identify, protect, and creatively use our center-point to give children the opportunity they need to absorb and activate Christian language for making meaning about life and death before they enter adolescence. This short term goal, however, is sometimes blurred when Godly Play moves into the mainstream of Christianity and its long-term goal, the maturity of child-like, graceful people, gets lost.

Ultimately, Godly Play's usefulness depends on being clear about its identity and yet supporting further diffusion and application. This may sound odd. How can diffusion, adaptation, and identity be part of the same vision? This is a necessary paradox. Godly Play needs to keep its foundational identity clear to continue stimulating creativity in the church's mainstream into which it is becoming assimilated. This means that Godly Players™ need to know very well who they are so they can work in all kinds of settings without becoming confused about what they are doing or confusing others about what Godly Play really is. This is also why Godly Play ® has been registered internationally as a trademark.

Diffusion and adaptation will now be discussed by providing ten examples of Godly Play diffusion and ten examples of adaptations to show that this complex vision is neither a pious dream nor a groundless enthusiasm. After looking at cases of diffusion and adaptation we will then suggest a way to keep Godly Play's identity clear by considering five levels of Godly Play involvement. First, however, let's begin with a story.

A Christmas Meeting in the Hills of Tennessee

The School of Theology at the University of the South in Sewanee, Tennessee, called a meeting of representatives from several groups working within in a broad interpretation of Montessori religious education at Christmastime around the turn of the last century. I knew all of these people, but they did not know each other. They needed to get acquainted so they could learn from and support each other.

Catechesis of the Good Shepherd was represented by Tina Lillig. Professor Sonja Stewart attended for Young Children and Worship. I represented Godly Play and Rosella Wiens Regier attended for Jubilee. Kay Weeks was present for what would become Children, Worship, and Wonder in the Christian Church (Disciples). The Reverend Ron Somers-Clark attended for the Dallas Children's Medical Center. Willa Brown represented the Reformed Church in America, which was and is involved in a "cooperative ministry" with the Christian Reformed Church in North America and the Presbyterian Church in Canada. The Reverend Dr. Dick Hardel represented the Youth and Family Institute, a program serving mostly Lutheran parishes.

The hospitality of the School of Theology was generous, and participants made presentations about their programs. We listened carefully to each other and discussed our hopes for children. No formal agreement resulted, nor was one intended. The goal was to meet face to face, because we seldom had a chance to be with each other to enjoy the larger tradition we shared. Our common commitment to children was enriched, so we left renewed to do our work in the ways we thought best. I am sorry to say that some of those wonderful people are now deceased or retired, but they have left a good heritage.

I know this book cannot be a substitute for such a meeting. My hope is, however, that the spirit of that Christmas meeting in the hills of Tennessee will find its way into the pages of this chapter.

Projects Branching Out from Godly Play

Godly Play's identity is clear. It consists of a theory, a method, a multi-volume spiral curriculum, and an awareness of the place of children in the history of theology.[1] Many people have found this body of work useful, so parts of *The Complete Guide To Godly Play* have been translated into or are being translated into Finnish, German, Spanish, Swahili, French, Swedish, Dutch, Chinese, Korean, and, perhaps, other languages. The early overview, *Godly Play*, was published in Korean on the twentieth anniversary of its first edition and the very early book, co-authored with Sonja Stewart, *Young Children and Worship*, has been translated into Japanese.

The Godly Play Foundation has strengthened this identity by providing training and support for teachers, fundraising, the manufacturing of teaching materials by Godly Play Resources, and research by the Center for the Theology of Childhood in Denver. It also supports Godly Play's development around the world by its relationships with the many national organizations and some thirty other interested groups. For example, in 2012 the fourth European Godly Play Conference, which meets every two years, was held in Germany and the annual National Godly Play Conference in Australia met for the second time. In 2013 the fifth North American Godly Play Conference was held in Toronto at Trinity College. This activity, combined with the many publications about Godly Play, suggests that it is well enough defined to contribute to the larger conversation about Christian education in the church. Since Godly Play began in 1974 many projects have branched out from its use of the Montessori tradition. Ten examples will be used to illustrate this diffusion into the mainstream of Christian education.

Young Children and Worship

The publication in 1989 of *Young Children and Worship* with Sonja Stewart helped encourage interest in Montessori religious education, especially in Protestant circles. The book began when Sonja Stewart came to Houston in 1985 with three of her graduate students to take one of the workshops I offered at Christ Church Cathedral. The next year I presented a workshop for her at Western Seminary in Holland, Michigan, where she was a professor of Christian education. *Young Children and Worship* grew out of these visits.

Professor Stewart began at once to offer her own workshops about young children and worship. In the summers she also offered major conferences at Western Seminary. I helped lead these twice. My role included presenting some Godly Play lessons, but mostly I led the afternoon sessions about classroom management since this part of her program was not yet developed.

The granddaughter of Sonja Stewart, the Reverend Olivia Stewart Robertson, is a Presbyterian minister and continues Sonja Stewart's work today. Dr. Stewart died from cancer on April 21, 2006, and is greatly missed.

Children and Worship: Reformed Church of America, Christian Reformed Church, and The Presbyterian Church of Canada

The Reformed Church in America, the Christian Reformed Church in North America, and the Presbyterian Church in Canada developed a "cooperative ministry" related to Sonja Stewart's interpretation of Godly Play and used *Young Children and Worship* as their basic text although they have developed additional materials to supplement this. Willa Brown was active in the development of this consortium when she was the associate for children's ministry for the Reformed Church in America. A team of teacher-trainers was organized, and during the early years I helped train new trainers at the invitation of the denominational office in Grand Rapids, Michigan.

Jubilee: The Anabaptist Tradition

Jubilee was inspired by Godly Play as well as by Sonja Stewart, Maria Harris, Mary Elizabeth Moore, and Walter Bruggeman. The executive director of this project was Rosella Wiens Regier. She and her team came to Houston several times to study the eight beautiful Godly Play rooms at Christ Church Cathedral and to attend workshops there. I was canon educator at the Cathedral from 1984 to 1994. Rosella told some of this story in the September 24, 1996, issue of *The Mennonite*.

Jubilee was created by six denominations representing the Anabaptist part of the Christian family: Brethren in Christ Church, Church of the Brethren, Friends United Meeting, General Conference Mennonite Church, Mennonite Brethren, and the Mennonite Church. They also produced training videos, curriculum materials, and hands-on teaching figures. Their wooden teaching materials were made by people in Central America and furnished to teachers in the United States through their missionaries.

Faith and Play: Quakers

The second Quaker offshoot from Godly Play is known as Faith and Play. It uses the core lessons of Godly Play but adds special lessons in the Godly Play style, developed specifically for the Quaker tradition. The Reverend Caryl Menkhus Creswell, who is a Quaker minister and a Godly Play trainer, has been the liaison between this group and the Godly Play Foundation.

Children, Wonder, and Worship: The Christian Church (Disciples)

The Christian Church (Disciples of Christ) interpretation of Godly Play has been guided by Kay Weeks. I was present with Kay and others on March 7, 2000, at Lexington Theological Seminary to dedicate a Godly Play room there. This was memorable for me, because the classroom was very beautiful and well cared for. It was also the first time I was asked to summarize my life's work in a five-minute homily. The worship service celebrating the opening of the new room was a joy to be part of. The Christian Church's approach is called "a Montessori influenced program" and their website links to the Godly Play Foundation.

Spirit Play: Unitarian Universalist

Dr. Nita Penfold developed Spirit Play for the Unitarian Universalist denomination, following the example of Godly Play. We became acquainted and worked together as I prepared to speak at the Boston General Assembly of the Unitarian Universalist Church some years ago. She developed what is called an "adaptation" of Godly Play that uses Montessori methods. This program offers training and is used by many Unitarian Universalist churches throughout the United States.

Jewish Godly Play

The term "Jewish Godly Play" is not quite right. All would agree. When I did Godly Play workshops at Leo Baeck College in London what I did was called simply "doing midrash with Jerome." The use of Godly Play principles in a Jewish context has also been called "Torah Play."

Rabbi Sandy Sasso and Rabbi Michael Shire have pioneered an adaptation of Godly Play for the Jewish world. In 2009 a discussion about the possibility of Jewish Godly Play was held in Denver with Rabbi Sasso and Rabbi Shire, who was then vice-principal of Leo Baeck College in London. He is now dean of the Schoolman Graduate School of Jewish Education and a professor of Jewish religious education at Hebrew College in Boston. New impetus for this project took place in 2012 during a workshop in Boston at All Saints Episcopal Church to explore this collaboration. Rabbi Dr. Shire led the workshop and was assisted by the Reverend Dr. Cheryl Minor, a Godly Play trainer. This was followed by a meeting in 2013 at Temple Isaiah in Boston at which I was present.

Deep Talk: Godly Play in Finnish Business Settings

Deep Talk grew out of Godly Play in Finland as the means to stimulate group discussion among adults in business settings. A Godly Play mentor leads a group of adults who gather to hear a story and "play" existential issues in relation to their work and home. Tuula Valkonen pioneered this work. She has worked with children for over thirty-five years and has been a consultant in both Finland and Africa. Juha Loudeslampi from the Institute of Religious Pedagogy in Jarvenpaa, Finland, is the program's consultant. This work was begun in 2010.

A Gift To the Child: A Multi-Religion Curriculum for Schools in the United Kingdom

Professor John Hull and his associates at the University of Birmingham in England developed a multi-religion program for schools directly influenced by the Godly Play method. Dr. Hull reported on this project in his 1996 article "A Gift to the Child: A New Pedagogy for Teaching Religion to Young Children," published in *Religious Education*.[2] This approach developed a hands-on approach with three-dimensional teaching aids, like Godly Play. In their terminology these materials were called *numens*.

The objects for teaching were defined by using three criteria. First, they needed to be a somewhat self-enclosed entity within the life and faith of a particular religion. Second, the object, such as the elephant Ganesha for Hindu children or a cross for Christians, needed to be charged with a sense of the sacred that draws one towards worship. Third, the object needed to be presented to the children as a "gift" for the making of religious meaning. Dr. Hull cited both Godly Play and Montessori religious education as foundational for this approach and I traveled to the University of Birmingham to consult with his team as the project was being developed.

India Sunday School Union: *Windows to Encounter* (Preschool to Grade Twelve)

The India Sunday School Union was formed in 1876 and has promoted Christian education, training, and curriculum resources in the region ever since. Dr. Ajit A. Prasadam is the general secretary and earned his Th.M. and Ph.D. at Princeton Theological Seminary. Professor James E. Loder was his primary advisor before Loder died in 2001. He also studied with James W. Fowler, when Fowler was a visiting professor at Princeton in 1993. Dr. Prasadam was instrumental in developing *Windows to Encounter,* as associate editor.

The ISSU curriculum *Windows to Encounter* consciously draws on Loder's theory of transformation and Godly Play. Dr. Elizabeth Frykberg, the chief editor, studied with James E. Loder and me, earning her Ph.D. from Princeton Seminary with Loder. She also taught Godly Play, utilizing *Young Children and Worship*, in her own church, as she drew out implications connecting Loder's theory for *Windows to Encounter.*

In this tacit way Godly Play influenced *Windows* from the very beginning.

The Godly Play Foundation and the ISSU began discussions in 2012 to see how they can work together to enhance *Windows* by using Godly Play materials, especially for kindergarten through the eighth grade. These talks have included how Godly Play materials might be manufactured in India.

This brief summary of the work with the ISSU concludes our examples of how Godly Play is being diffused into the mainstream of Christian education. We now turn to another group of examples. They will show the variety of ways that Godly Play has been adapted for special settings. Each example is a project of a Godly Play trainer, so the level of Godly Play is strong, but the setting requires adjustment, which can confuse the onlooker about what is and is not Godly Play. Sometimes the *outgrowths* from Godly Play and the *adaptations* of Godly Play overlap, which also adds to the confusion.

Adaptations of Godly Play for Special Situations

There is much to be learned from the branches that have grown out from Godly Play. There is also much to be learned from the adaptations that have been made for special settings, even though they may not be fully-rounded examples of Godly Play at work. We turn now to ten examples.

Godly Play in Churches

Godly Play done in a church setting is the most widespread use for Godly Play in the United States. Many Christian educators have experimented creatively with the "forty-five minute hour" on Sunday morning and in addition have tried to find ways for children to engage in Godly Play in other settings and at other times, such as after school during the week or on Saturdays.

This kind of adaptation has been going on since the beginning. Thea and I met with children on Saturdays for our research classes in various places in Houston for about thirty years. We offered two-hour classes for younger children in the morning and two-hour classes for older children in the afternoons. We found that when we treated these sessions like other first-rate classes for children in the city—such as ballet, music, sports, etc.—they were more respected. We charged the same top fees that the best art classes did, so our research classes not only paid for themselves but made the point that the art of making meaning with Christian language is as worthy of respect as any of the other arts.

Godly Play in Schools

Godly Play was also involved in schools from the beginning. I went each Advent for over thirty years to School of the Woods, a Montessori school in Houston, to present the Godly Play Advent story to each of the classes. I was also chaplain at Holy Spirit Episcopal School in Houston for two years. These experiences showed the possibilities for Godly Play in schools, but an example of how this potential has been fully met is Rosemary Beales's current program at St. Stephens and St. Agnes School in Alexandria, Virginia. She built an airy, bright, and beautiful Godly Play room that is a pleasure to sit in and learn from, but she has done much more. The children are engaged in worship and service projects as well as their religion classes. In addition she has developed a program for parents.

Dr. Beales's six-week "Nurturing the Nurturers" project helps parents gain confidence and skills to become their children's primary spiritual mentors and to involve their families in a more active sharing of spiritual practices together. The program has been very successful and beneficial to both children and their families. This project was Dr. Beales's D.Min. thesis at Virginia Theological Seminary, so detailed information is available at Virginia Theological Seminary's Bishop Payne Library.

Godly Play in Homes

Old paintings of family worship show the serious, bearded father reading from the Bible in the parlor by the fire or children and parents kneeling to say their prayers by the bed before going to sleep. Today it is more likely for families to gather at most once a week during special seasons in the church year around the table to pray and prepare for such celebrations as Christmas and Easter.

There are four Godly Play lessons presently available for the family table and for other occasions. They are Advent, Lent, Creation, and The Good Shepherd. The materials are smaller than those used in the Godly Play room and the lessons are briefer, but they are similar enough that children will recognize them as old friends. The example that follows is for Lent. It has been chosen because keeping a holy Lent is often overlooked in Christian homes today.

The material includes seven small wooden plaques illustrated with the face of Christ at different times in his life. They fit in a beautiful box created by Godly Play Resources that also holds a felt strip divided into six purple and one white section by gold, wooden markers. This is a smaller version of the material used for "The Faces of Easter."[3] It is designed to be kept with other family treasures for Easter in a china cabinet or elsewhere. The presentation needs to be firmly but informally led, so everyone can relax and follow the ritual with a sense of humor and seriousness in about equal parts.

The felt underlay is unrolled section by section as Lent progresses, so the image for the day can be placed on it. The first week the Christ Child is laid on the purple underlay and the family wonders about birth stories. The second Sunday the face of Jesus, as an older child, is placed on the underlay and the family wonders about being lost and found, as Jesus was in the Temple. The third Sunday is Jesus' baptism and family baptisms are remembered. The fourth Sunday Jesus' time in the desert is evoked and the family wonders about what kind of work they are called to do. On the fifth Sunday of Lent Jesus' work is remembered as coming so close to people that they are healed and that he told parables, finally becoming one. The wondering is about how people in the family help those who are sick and what it is like to ponder parables. On the sixth Sunday the family remembers how Jesus shared the bread and wine with the disciples during Holy Week. The family tells stories about their memories of participating in Holy Communion.

On Easter Sunday the underlay turns from purple to white. The tile placed on the underlay has the face of the crucified Christ on one side and the resurrected Christ on the other. The two sides cannot be pulled apart. When you see one side you know the other is always there and that is the mystery of Easter. The family then tells stories about Easters they remember.

The Godly Play lessons for the family table and other occasions connect the family story with the Great Story. This gives children and adults a chance for the mutual blessing of remembering who they are and where they have come from, so they can know better where they are going.

Godly Play and Empirical Research

The research aspect of Godly Play is expanding in several countries, so I will mention only two examples, which are related.

Dr. Rebecca Nye is a child psychologist and Godly Play trainer in England. She worked with Dr. David Hay, a biologist and theologian, to publish *The Spirit of the Child,* which conceptualized children's spirituality as "relational consciousness."[4] This concept is "a framework for children's spirituality" that includes the "dimensions of this core category," "contexts," "conditions," "strategies," "process," and "consequences." The larger context for this research project was provided by Dr. Hay with commentary in several chapters while Dr. Nye did the empirical research and wrote the chapters about it.

In the United States, another Godly Play trainer, the Reverend Dr. Cheryl Minor, wrote her Ph.D. thesis about "Promoting Spiritual Well-Being: A Quasi-Experimental Test of Hay and Nye's Theory of Children Spirituality." Her study used Hay and Nye's theory to study whether or not Godly Play promoted spiritual well being and what its continuing effects might be. Her sample was 183 children, ages five to twelve years, enrolled in Godly Play. The stability of the effect was measured by a sample of forty children from ten to twelve years who had left Godly Play programs. The relationship between exposure to the program and well-being was tentatively established, but the most interesting feature of this study was that the beneficial effect did not often appear until after the older children had left the program.

Godly Play and Dementia

Several Godly Play trainers and mentors have also been working in this field. In the United Kingdom the two leaders are Alison Seaman, a Godly Play trainer and a free-lance advisor and consultant in spiritual education, and Richard Allen, an Anglican priest and full-time mental health chaplain. A paper they have written concerning care for dementia and Godly Play is on the website of Godly Play: UK at "Godly Play for Other Contexts/Ages."

In the United States Dr. Kelly O'Shea Carney, executive director, and the Reverend Scott Brooks Cope, director of pastoral care, are beginning a program related to Godly Play at the Phoebe Center for Excellence in Dementia Care in Allentown, Pennsylvania. Before working with older people Chaplain Cope was the senior chaplain at Wolfson Children's Hospital in Jacksonville, Florida, where they continue to use Godly Play in their pastoral care department. Sally Thomas in Denver is also interested in this field. She is a nurse, a certified spiritual director, and a Godly Play trainer.

The Reverend Lois Howard has been working the longest in this field in the United States. She is an Episcopal deacon, a Godly Play trainer, and a professional clown. Her team of six trained volunteers in Lexington, Kentucky, meets on Mondays with about twenty-four "Alzheimer's folks," as she lovingly calls them, in a residential center. The participants and the volunteers wonder together about a presentation, selected from a rotation of twelve stories that have been found most effective. Games are also played and there is singing. The staff has reported that the participants are much calmer the rest of the day.

On Wednesdays Reverend Howard brings a group of preschool children to visit with about a dozen Alzheimer people attending an adult day care center. The children sit with the older people for a Godly Play presentation and they sing. There are lots of hugs and kisses. In this case the staff reported that Wednesday is the only time in the week when the participants continue smiling most of the day. The children have also reported that they enjoy these visits and feel good about their contribution to the lives of these older people.

Godly Play and Children in Hospitals

Godly Play grew out of experiences with sick children and their families in hospitals. This included Thea's and my own children, especially Coleen, and my professional involvement with children most notably at Texas Children's Hospital and M. D. Anderson in Houston's Texas Medical Center. A program for hospital chaplains and for family therapy using Godly Play was developed during the decade I worked in the Texas Medical Center, 1974 to 1984, but little of that initiative has survived.

What disappeared in Houston, however, became institutionalized at Dallas Children's Medical Center, where Godly Play has been used for over a quarter of a century as part of their pastoral care and Clinical Pastoral Education (CPE) training for pediatric chaplains. Ron Somers-Clark was chaplain and director of pastoral care when they began to use Godly Play and upon his retirement his successor Chaplain Doug Watts has continued to expand their research and clinical practice.

In 1992 an issue of *Childtimes: Children's Medical Center of Dallas* discussed their Godly Play program. Two of the pictures in the article show children on the floor working with Godly Play materials in their newly constructed chapel. The chaplains in Dallas have used carts with art supplies and Godly Play materials as well as other means, such as the hospital video system, to make Godly Play available. A Godly Play room adjoins the chapel in Dallas and on the Plano campus, north of Dallas, a new chapel was built in 2012 that was also inspired by Godly Play. A Godly Play trainer, Andy Rosane, who is a painter and Montessori teacher, and I were consultants.

In hospitals the use of Godly Play goes beyond the care of children and their families. Since the opening of the Godly Play room in Dallas Children's Medical Center, staff groups who have participated in a Godly Play circle include: nurse interns from the critical care units, radiology interns, child life specialists, the Funnyactrics Clown therapy group, and staff from the foundation/development office. In addition, on March 18, 2013, the Pastoral Care Department presented an interdisciplinary symposium about children's spirituality and health. This was through the department's newly created Center for the Spirituality of Children, founded in 2012. Both Chaplain Watts and Chaplain Ryan Campbell, the manager of the Center for the Spirituality of Children, are graduates of The General Theological Seminary certificate program for the spiritual guidance of children and are Godly Play trainers.

Children with Handicaps

When Godly Play was being developed, especially from 1974 to 1984, I worked closely with the chaplains in the mental health and mental retardation institutions in the state of Texas, but today the person with the most experience working with children who have special needs is Dr. Wolfhard Schweiker in Germany. He has a double competency with a doctor's degree in Christian education and a master's degree in theology and special education. He is also a pastor and has been a teacher at the Special School in Moessingen. He now teaches at the Center for Theology and Education of the Protestant Church of Wuerttemberg (Lutheran Confession) in Stuttgart and at Ludwigsburg University of Education. He also has published widely and is a Godly Play trainer.

In 2008 Dr. Schweiker gave a lecture for the fourth North American Godly Play Conference at the Church Divinity School of the Pacific in Berkeley, California. He challenged the conference to ask how to include children with special needs in Godly Play circles. During the succeeding years, he has reframed this view to say that *all people are different*, so it is better to say that *all children* should be included. What we share is our differentness. A second commonality is that we are all "vulnerable and mortal. It is only in God that we may find identification and solidarity." In addition to his academic teaching Dr. Schweiker continues to initiate and supervise practical projects for "inclusive religious education."

General Pastoral Care

Dr. Rebecca Nye has been asked often in the United Kingdom to comment on the pastoral care of children. This is because of her work with David Hay on *The Spirit of the Child* and in 2002 she was one of the three authors of *Psychology for Christian Ministry* with the lead author Fraser Watts and Sara Savage. She found that the main problem with responding to such requests has been that the definition of *pastoral care* is too broad and fuzzy, so she developed her own definition as the care of children's "*well*-being." Another limit to her response has been the paucity of references to children in the general literature of pastoral care. This is clearly an area that needs to be developed and is a project she is helping with.

In the United States some foundational work has been done concerning the pastoral care of children. During the 1980s Dr. Andrew D. Lester of Brite Divinity School wrote *Pastoral Care with Children in Crisis* concerning the pastoral neglect of children and the use of play, art, and storytelling to provide care.[5] He also edited *A Sourcebook for Ministry with Children in Crisis* a few years later dealing with such issues as divorce, bereavement, hospitalization, terminal illness, chronic illness, abuse, disability, stress, and anxiety.[6] Neither of these books involved Godly Play explicitly, but the use of an art bag and Lester's playfulness made his approach a kindred spirit.

Lester's work shaped the writing of a manual about the pastoral care of children that I wrote for the Community of Hope, which was used privately by the community and was introduced at one of their early conferences at Camp Allen near Houston in the 1990s. The Community of Hope is an international volunteer lay pastoral care ministry founded by the Reverend Dr. Helen Appleberg. It grew out of the pastoral care department at St. Luke's Hospital in Houston, but has been independent now for several decades.

The Playing Church

Juha Luodeslampi's many publications are mostly in Finnish. One booklet in English, however, invites the church to become playful like children. In 2005 the Finnish Evangelical Lutheran Parishes' Centre for Child Work published *Church at Play: A Finnish Approach to Christian Upbringing and Spirituality* by Emilia Kosunen and Juha Luodeslampi.[7] The picture of a child running down the central aisle of a church, looking up with bright eyes, is almost reason enough to find this publication. The booklet developed the concept of "the playing church" and invited children and adults to take part. It was not specifically about Godly Play, but it was clearly informed by Godly Play. Juha Luodeslampi is a leader among Godly Play mentors in Finland and is a trainer. Finland is known internationally as the leader in schools and social services for children, Finnish was the first foreign language that *The Complete Guide To Godly Play* was translated into.

Godly Play and Adult Education

There has also been an interest in Godly Play as adult education since the beginning. After all, there are echoes from the sixth-century *Lectio Divina* for adults in it. During workshops in the late 1970s and 1980s lessons were presented to adults like they were to children so the participants could feel what children feel and because I wanted to see if there were artificial language ceilings or walls limiting the lessons for adults. Regularly, during the late mornings or early afternoons someone would observe, "Couldn't this work with adults?" All I could say was, "Hasn't it been working with you?"

It is important for storytellers to be able to participate in the lessons *as adults* to convey nonverbally their own involvement with the creative process. If this does not happen then the unspoken teaching is that the lesson is not important or worth wondering about for adults. The most important thing the storyteller has to teach is to show how to be authentically involved and to honestly wonder with God and the community of children.

Godly Play was connected with adult education from the beginning in another way. When it came time to think about training trainers for Godly Play I consulted with the Reverend Dr. Edward De Bary and other leaders in the Education for Ministry (EfM) program, an Episcopal adult education initiative begun in 1975. Their approach to education was similar in spirit to Godly Play, but they had much more experience in organization and training trainers, so we began to work together. A few years later when Godly Play was introduced to Australia it was sometimes called "EfM for children." EfM is active in many countries, but its hub is at the School of Theology, which is part of the University of the South, located at Sewanee, Tennessee. Today there is a growing crossover in leadership between EfM and Godly Play. Dr. De Bary led the way by serving a term as a board member for the organization that became the Godly Play Foundation.

This description of ten applications of Godly Play in different contexts can now be added to the ten examples of programs stimulated by Godly Play. So many illustrations can cause vertigo, so let's discuss how to keep Godly Play's identity clear in such a mix.

Identity and Diffusion without Confusion

When Godly Play began about forty years ago it was almost impossible for people other than Thea and me to see the whole vision. We knew where we were going by intuition, but mostly we just enjoyed what we were doing and did it for itself, enjoying the company of children and each other. As time passed more and more people began to look over our shoulders, so we started the arduous process of writing for and training others. Today the vision is well documented, so Godly Play's identity can be maintained, but it may be helpful to think together about people's interest in Godly Play as levels of involvement.

The first level is *Ideal Godly Play*. There are five areas of mastery needed to do Godly Play in an optimum way. First, one needs to know the foundational literature. Books and articles about the theory, method, spiral curriculum, and the theological context for Godly Play are available as well as follow-up materials used in the core trainings. This literature is summarized in Volume 8 of *The Complete Guide To Godly Play*.[8] Knowing Godly Play principles is important because they can guide mentors when what takes place is beyond their experience. Knowing *why* helps knowing *how*.

The second area of mastery needed for *Ideal Godly Play* is to be able to engage in the process fluently. This is the focus of the core trainings. The structure of the class, classroom management (supporting the community of children and their creativity), learning a few beginning lessons well and presenting one or more to the group in order to experience feedback and gain confidence are all involved. One also needs to know how to work in triads to practice, so that the triad—presenting, focused listening, and critical observation—becomes part of one's imagination for self-growth. The awareness of the middle realm is one of the most important discoveries that these core trainings offer. This is mostly taught nonverbally.

It is very helpful to take several core trainings with different trainers to confirm what is unique to mentors and where classical consistency lies. The core training is not the end of one's preparation. It is the beginning. The Godly Play Foundation is developing continuing education modules and more advanced core trainings. For example a series of workshops in the United States about the new lessons in Volume 8 of *The Complete Guide To Godly Play* is now available.

A third area of mastery has two parts. One needs to learn all the lessons. This takes a long time, because it needs to be done while working with children and other mentors, using the volumes of *The Complete Guide*. Progress can be checked by reference to the outline of the curriculum in the Appendix of Volume 8 of *The Complete Guide*.

An *awareness* of the curriculum as a whole is also important, even if all the lessons have not been learned. One of the best ways to accomplish this is to participate in the two practicum courses at The General Theological Seminary in New York City that are part of the courses for the Certificate in the Spiritual Guidance of Children. It takes eighty hours to experience the whole curriculum. This is not done to become fluent in each lesson but to become aware of the language system as a whole, to notice the many interconnections among the presentations, and to get a sense of the broad themes that run through the whole spiral.

A fourth area of mastery involves broadening one's view of Godly Play by cross-training. It is helpful to take the Montessori training and to become involved in Catechesis of the Good Shepherd to understand the larger Montessori tradition out of which Catechesis and Godly Play come. My Montessori training was in Italy in 1972 to 1973 and my Catechesis training was with Cavalletti in 1978 in Houston. I also took a refresher course after she was no longer training. The course was excellent. There is a third kind of cross-training that can also be useful. It is to participate in the Education for Ministry (EfM) program from the School of Theology in Sewanee, Tennessee. One might even become a mentor or trainer of mentors, as a few Godly Players in the United States and Australia have done.

The fifth area of mastery for *Ideal Godly Play* is to seek as much experience as possible. How much experience does it takes to be a Godly Play mentor? This is an interesting question, because in churches "experience" usually means about an hour a week in direct contact with children. If classes meet about fifty times a year this equals approximately fifty hours. In weekday schools the contact with children is roughly forty hours *a week* or a little less. The lack of opportunities for contact with children in the church is why Thea and I continued to work in Montessori schools while Godly Play was being developed and Thea continued the rest of her life to teach in a Montessori school, developing her music classes and her after-school music program. As with any art, practicing one's art is indispensible to being an artist.

Developing the above five areas of mastery is daunting. It sounds almost impossible, but it is the ideal. This is what Thea and I did, filling in bits and pieces over many decades to continue improving our art, which we loved doing well. There are, however, other levels of involvement.

Good Enough Godly Play is named after Winnicott's "good enough mothering." This refers to when a mother's attunement with her infant is no longer complete and she begins to approximate meeting her baby's needs. As she re-enters the adult world "good enough mothering" begins, which is good for both the mother and the infant.

Good Enough Godly Play does not encompass the whole vision that *Ideal Godly Play* does, but it still aspires to complete that ideal. People working at this level know what they do not yet know. One cannot always devote all the time and energy one might like to Godly Play, much like in good enough mothering, so one does what one can. People providing *Good Enough Godly Play* to children as spiritual guidance are still aware, like in *Ideal Godly Play,* that they are receiving spiritual guidance from children, which enables them to continue to grow in their art and to be continually refreshed in their theological play. They also seek out continuing education and understand that learning the art of Godly Play is a lifelong process. *Good Enough Godly Play* is a compromise between the ideal and the possible but the compromise is made only for the moment, as one keeps learning.

Good Enough Godly Play is where many Godly Players are. Their rooms aren't quite what they would like, but they know what is missing and what needs improvement. They understand that their fluency in the whole corpus of the lessons is still limited but they know how to get to the level of fluency they desire and they are working at it. To be more specific, *Good Enough Godly Play* involves mastery of about three-quarters of *Ideal Godly Play's* five categories: foundational knowledge, training in the process, awareness of the whole curriculum, cross training, and experience. Leaders lead by showing how, so ways are found to work directly with children, despite sometimes very heavy organizational responsibilities.

Okay Godly Play is the third level of involvement. It engages about half of the theory and practice and often involves mixing

Godly Play with other approaches. The awareness of and participation in the middle realm and the rest of the process is also about half of that in *Ideal Godly Play* and is inconsistent. Leaders often do not lead from experience or extensive training in Godly Play at this level. The aspiration to know more about Godly Play is also less than in *Good Enough Godly Play.*

Okay Godly Play is often based on an informed decision that balances many conflicts to define this level of involvement. Such things as the training needed, the cost involved, the responsibility for spiritual guidance rather than education in a narrow sense, the need to relate to adults as an administrator rather than be with the children, an uncertainty about Montessori education in general, and other considerations make *Ideal Godly Play* or *Good Enough Godly Play* unreasonable for a particular setting. At this level there is more interest in a workable compromise than continuing to pursue the ideal. This is the level of Godly Play in many of the branches that have grown out of Godly Play.

When involvement falls below *Okay Godly Play* associating the name "Godly Play" with the program is deceptive. Let's call the fourth level *Godly Play In Name Only.* This approach may actually use a different *method*, which only vaguely looks like Godly Play. Some of the same materials might be used, or materials that look like Godly Play materials to the untutored eye. A book of lessons may be organized like those found in *The Complete Guide To Godly Play*, but when the material is read it becomes clear that it is dominated by a chaotic assembly of word searches, teacher-directed art projects, cartoon pictures to color, matching exercises, competitive games for memorizing scripture, and other such educational strategies that work against the theory and practice of Godly Play.

This level of involvement includes little of the foundational knowledge or the ability to engage in the Godly Play process. Experience is problematic, whether extensive or not, because it is not related to Godly Play mentoring.

A fifth level, *Anti-Godly Play*, can actually be dangerous for children's spirituality. I have seen some programs that appear to be like Godly Play because the children are introduced in a warm and welcoming way, but after the playfulness of the invitation the process shifts to one that is controlling and manipulative. The goal is to tell children how to think and feel about God and to teach an authoritarian, other-directed quality of religious experience. *Anti-Godly Play* takes advantage of children's lack of social awareness and self-direction. They are taught to swallow their questions, extinguish their wonder, and become mindless mimics of Christian life and language.

One day I received a book of lessons with a cheery, bright cover that showed wooden figures like those used in Godly Play. The lessons were laid out like Godly Play lessons, but the content was based on a one-way, transfer model of education that was limited to teaching church and biblical "facts." Adult, doctrinal interpretations were learned about scripture rather than wondering about scripture itself. Each lesson had a summary that was to be parroted correctly before moving on to the next lesson. This was created with the best possible motives to be like Godly Play, but it was antithetical.

Godly Play needs to be part of the continued scanning for a better way for children to become part of the Christian community and language domain. At the same time it needs to keep its composure while making a soft closure about its identity. It cannot make a contribution if it does not understand its own identity and know how to communicate it clearly.

The Transition To The Next Generation

As Godly Play moves into the fifth generation, it is engaging with new themes in children's spirituality. Philip Sheldrake will be our guide to these emerging themes. His thirty years of teaching and scholarship in this field, which he helped create, will help give shape to this future.[9] At the end of the twentieth century, "the Christian approach to and experience of spirituality was more varied, eclectic, global, ecumenical, and radically plural than at almost any point in the history of Christianity."[10] In the second decade of the new millennium this diversity has increased. The "post-Christian era," however, seems to be giving way to the "the post-secular" era, because of this wide interest in spirituality. Six themes are becoming evident.

The first theme involves global consciousness. What we eat, wear, worry about, and link to electronically is implicitly if not explicitly involved in a worldwide network, so our spirituality is as well. This means that Christianity needs to be more deeply rooted than ever before and yet open at the same time. The spirit of playful orthodoxy, which is stimulated by the way Christian language is learned, is a primary characteristic of Godly Play. This awareness of how Godly Play is related to interreligious understanding needs to be strengthened in the future.

A second theme to be conscious of is how spirituality is related to our planet's needs. The speed and ease of modern travel has transformed the earth from a vast, undiscovered place to one that is crowded and shrinking. In the past the planet could be mistreated and still heal itself, but not today. This crisis makes ecology an undeniable part of spirituality, which is of deep concern for Godly Play.

The open space of the Godly Play room acquaints children with cleaning up their own spills, repairing broken materials, keeping the environment clean, and putting things back where they belong when they are no longer in use. These and other such habits become spiritual practices and translate into caring for the larger environment, but more can be done. The place to start, however, is with the consciousness of this theme in the Godly Play room. This does not necessarily mean that one ought to create lessons about the spirituality of nature, but it is important to be open to nature in all of one's wondering and care of the Godly Play room. What can be done in addition to this will come out of deepening this awareness.

A third theme is to rebalance the concerned active life, committed to justice, with contemplation. Contemplation is as important for ethical activists as activism is for contemplatives, because this kind of consciousness brings the largest perspective possible—a God's eye view—to our experience about how to live together well. Nourishing an awareness of the limits to our being and knowing is important for an adequate ethical response to guide our daily lives.

For example, in the Godly Play room we do not step on children's work. Children working on the floor with paints, clay, and other materials respect each other because even though they are working on their own expressive art projects about personal, existential concerns, there is still a feeling in the middle realm of working together. To step on another's work is like stepping on your own creativity. With this kind of awareness the mentor can nourish the unity between contemplation and ethical action.

A fourth theme that is emerging is contemplation without walls. As older religious communities decline, the interest in spirituality, once protected and supported there, is being lived out in other kinds of communities in the world. The spirituality and practice of classical communities such as the Benedictines,

Dominicans, and Franciscans is still needed for inspiration and guidance, but what these ancient communities know is now needed everywhere more than ever.

The emphasis on contemplative silence in the Godly Play room prepares children for spirituality without walls. There is not even a designated "prayer corner" in a Godly Play room. Instead, contemplative silence permeates everything that is done, from carrying materials from the shelves to the circle and replacing them when finished, to the spaces between the words in the presentation, and the slow, deliberate rituals when children arrive and when they depart. The whole process, including the laughter and tears, is infused with contemplation.

A fifth contemporary theme is the engagement between spirituality and creativity. This has been emphasized during the last two chapters of this book, but Sheldrake has provided a short list of significant areas of research where this cooperation is critical. He noted that "quantum physics, genetic research, neuroscience, artificial intelligence, cyberspace, and cosmology do not simply raise ethical issues or philosophical-theological questions."[11] These fields involve researchers, mostly unequipped for such reflection, in questions that challenge our assumptions about the nature of humankind and what the purpose of life truly is. How these questions are faced and discussed openly will stimulate "unexpected ways to encounter the numinous" in the future for both children and adults.

Few of us have the command of art, science, and religion that Copernicus had to create a new vision of the cosmos, but like the church of his day we need to be more involved in making spiritual breadth and depth a greater priority. The church is uniquely equipped to engage spirituality with the creative process, but the place to begin is not just with adults. The place to begin is with the youngest children, as Godly Play does.

Finally, there is a theme of spirituality that Sheldrake did not mention. It is one that has been largely ignored by the church over the centuries, but is emphasized by this book. Spiritual maturity involves becoming like a child, which in turn involves the mutual blessing of adults and children. This is a core value of Godly Play, but it also needs to become the center of the church's concern, as we make our way forward.

A Blessing for the Journey

When Charles Dickens ended *A Christmas Carol* he asked Tiny Tim to help him conclude. The child had, after all, helped transform old Scrooge into someone who knew how to keep Christmas well. It is as if Dickens and Tiny Tim are standing together at the end of the book blessing each other. They then turn to us, the readers, and bless us, to send us on our way to keep Christmas like a new Scrooge. Tiny Tim put this into words, speaking for himself and the author, "God Bless Us, Every One."[12]

As *this* book concludes, the author also invites a child to join him. This child is on the cover of the book and is himself. We bless each other and then turn to you with our mutual blessing to send you on your way. But shouldn't there be more? Can such a blessing be allowed to fall silent, trapped between the covers of a book?

Why not continue the blessing? This can be done quietly in your church. Invite a child to stand beside the one who pronounces the blessing at the end of worship. There is no rubric nor theological principle I know of that objects to a child standing silently beside the one who gives the blessing. It is little trouble to arrange for each child in the parish to take a turn. There is no expense. There is only this simple act.

When the "blessing child" is selected each week, she or he can be prepared by saying that children don't need to do anything to bless. They bless by standing there and being who they are. You don't need to make any gesture, like the adult does, because children *are* the gesture.

The adult leader proceeds as usual with the blessing, but nonverbally it is no longer one-way communication. It flows between the child and the adult, then it is *that mutual blessing* which flows out into the congregation and returns to the Creator. This draws the generations of the congregation into its circle, giving and receiving blessings to become blessings.

There is nothing new about this. It is a parable of action, like Jesus did for the disciples and us. It evokes the need to become like a child to enter his realm and to welcome children to know him. These sayings are connected to each other and to the mutual blessing of the generations. You can't become child-like if you never welcome children.

Being blessed by mutual blessing can release the original grace we were born with. That is the only risk involved. Who knows what will happen if gracefulness overwhelms the church?

notes

Chapter 1

1. Gabriel Moran, *Showing How: The Act of Teaching* (Valley Forge, PA: Trinity Press, 1997), 219–225.

2. J. B. Phillips, *Your God Is Too Small* (New York: Touchstone Books 2004), 75–86.

3. Jerome W. Berryman, *Children and the Theologians: Clearing the Way for Grace* (New York: Morehouse, 2009), 197.

4. Books reflecting this change include Kristin Herzog, *Children and Our Global Future: Theological and Social Challenges* (Cleveland, OH: Pilgrim Press, 2005); Marcia J. Bunge, ed. *The Child in the Bible*, with the assistance of Terrence E. Fretheim and Beverly Roberts Gaventa (Grand Rapids, MI: Wm. B. Erdmans Publishing Company, 2008); and Don S. Browning and Marcia J. Bunge, eds., *Children and Childhood in World Religions: Primary Sources and Texts* (New Brunswick, NJ: Rutgers University Press, 2009).

5. Steven Mithen, *The Prehistory of the Mind: A Search for the Origins of Art, Religion and Science* (London: Phoenix, 1996), 69–78.

6. Mithen, *Prehistory of Mind*, 36.

7. Mithen, *Prehistory of Mind*, 173.

8. James E. Reed and Ronnie Prevost, *A History of Christian Education* (Nashville, TN: Broadman & Holman, 1993), 257.

9. Hugh Cunningham, *The Invention of Childhood* (London: BBC Books, 2006), 131.

10. John L. Elias, *A History of Christian Education: Protestant, Catholic, and Orthodox Perspectives* (Malabar, FL: Krieger, 2002), 166.

11. Elias, *A History of Christian Education*, 166.

12. Elias, *A History of Christian Education*, 166.

13. John H. Westerhoff III, *Will Our Children Have Faith?* 3rd ed. (New York: Morehouse, 2012), 52–79 for community and 89–105 for faith development.

14. A phrase generally attributed to Westerhoff.

15. John H. Westerhoff and O. C. Edwards, *A Faithful Church: Issues in the History of Catechesis* (Wilton, CT: Morehouse-Barlow, 1981), v.

16. Westerhoff and Edwards, *A Faithful Church*, 4–5.

17. Diana Butler Bass, *Christianity After Religion: The End of Church and the Birth of a New Spiritual Awakening* (New York: HarperCollins, 2012), 201–214.

18. Dava Sobel, *A More Perfect Heaven: How Copernicus Revolutionized the Cosmos* (New York: Walker, 2012), 3–79.

Chapter 2

1. Anna M. Maccheroni, *A True Romance: Doctor Maria Montessori as I Knew Her* (Edinburgh: Darien Press, 1947); E. M. Standing, *Maria Montessori: Her Life and Work* (New York: Plume, 1984); Rita Kramer, *Maria Montessori: A Biography*, with Foreword by Anna Freud (Reading, MA: Addison Wesley, 1988); Phyllis Povell, *Montessori Comes to America: The Leadership of Maria Montessori and Nancy McCormick Rambusch* (Lanham, MD: University Press of America, 2010). Povell's work draws largely on Valeria P. Babini and Luisa Lama's *Una "Donna Nuova:" Il femminismo scientifico di Maria Montessori* (Milan: FrancoAngeli, 2003). In addition to these written sources, I have incorporated the oral tradition that was part of the training course in Bergamo, Italy, where I studied from 1971 to 1972 at the *Centro Internazionale Studi Montessoriani*. Mario Montessori founded the school in 1961 and was still part of the faculty when I was a student.

2. Kramer, *Maria Montessori*, Preface. Kramer, who comes to Montessori-based Christian education from a Jewish background, is also "more complicated and interesting" than her single book about Montessori might otherwise suggest.

3. Kramer, *Maria Montessori*, 24. Maria's mother, Renilde Stoppani, was herself a well-read, independent woman, whose choice of names for Maria may have influenced her non-traditional path. Renilde's uncle, the scholar-priest and poet Antonio Stoppani, who integrated science and religion in his own work, probably also influenced Maria's education and career choices.

Maria's full name was Maria Tecla Artemisia Montessori. Tecla (also Thecla) was the fiercely independent woman of gnostic legend who renounced the traditional path of marriage and children in order to follow St. Paul. The name Artemisia was either a reference to the Greek goddess of the forests and of childbirth or to the groundbreaking baroque artist Artemisia Gentileschi. Povell, *Montessori Comes to America*, 27–29.

4. Kramer, *Maria Montessori*, 94.

5. Kramer, *Maria Montessori*, 46.

6. Povell, *Montessori Comes to America*, 32.

7. Povell, *Montessori Comes to America*, 30–31. Povell's research indicates that "many" women were practicing medicine prior to Unification in 1870. After Unification, when society became more conservative, a number of women still graduated with medical degrees before Montessori, including Edvige Benigni and Marcellina Corio Viola, who graduated from the University of Rome in 1890 and 1894, respectively. Montessori's accomplishment is still significant, even if she wasn't the very first woman to graduate with a medical degree from an Italian university.

8. Povell, *Montessori Comes to America*, 36.

9. Referred to as "scientific feminism," by Babini and Lama, *Una Donna Nuova*.

10. Maria Montessori, *The Montessori Method*, trans. Anne E. George (New York: Schocken Books, 1970), 36.

11. Montessori, *Method*, 36.

12. Giuseppe Montesano (1861–1961) is considered one of the founders of child psychiatry in Italy. Montesano acknowledged his son legally shortly before his marriage to Maria Aprile on October 6, 1901. However, Montessori usually referred to Mario as her nephew or "adopted son," until just before her death, when she named him in her will. This formal acknowledgment facilitated the transfer of Montessori's wealth

and the leadership of the movement to Mario upon Maria's death. Kramer, *Maria Montessori*, 368–369.

13. Kramer, *Maria Montessori*, 24.

14. Montessori, *Method*, 230.

15. Montessori, *Method*, 376.

16. A child's spiritual nature is not always obvious. One day a little girl of about three was fitting graded cylinders into their proper places in a wooden container. She kept taking them out, mixing them up, and then replacing them over and over. Montessori counted forty-two repetitions. Even though Montessori tried, the child could not be distracted until she had "finished." Before this Montessori had not realized that children had such powers of concentration. She thought this power was almost like the meditation of the mystics.

Another day Montessori brought a four-month-old baby girl into class with her. The children watched the silent infant with rapt attention. This was the origin of the silence game, later a classical part of the Montessori curriculum, which is also like meditation. Montessori had realized that children love and need silence. Maria Montessori, *The Discovery of the Child*, trans. M. Joseph Costelloe (Notre Dame: Fides, 1967), 145–146, 150–53.

17. Montessori, *Discovery of the Child*, 37.

18. Mario Montessori, "Dr. Maria Montessori and the Child" in *The Spiritual Hunger of the Modern Child, A Series of Ten Lectures* (Charles Town, West Virginia: Claymont Communications, 1984), 50–51; Maria Montessori, *The Secret of Childhood* (Notre Dame, Indiana: Fides Publishers, Inc., 1970, Dome Edition), 140–141. The quotation is not exact. He may have been freely translating from an Italian edition or embellishing what was written in *The Secret of Childhood*.

19. Montessori, *Method*, 371.

20. Montessori, *Method*, 372.

21. Montessori, *Method*, 82.

22. Montessori, *Discovery of the Child*, 179.

23. Montessori, *Method*, 13.

24. Maria Montessori, et al., *The Child in the Church*, ed. E. M. Standing (St Paul, MN: Catechetical Guild, 1965) 88–89.

25. Standing, *Maria Montessori*, 69.

26. Montessori, et al., *The Child in the Church*, 22.

27. Kramer, *Maria Montessori*, 177.

28. Povell, *Montessori Comes to America*, 105.

29. Kramer, *Maria Montessori*, 250.

30. Montessori, et al., *The Child in the Church*, Chapters 2–5.

31. Kramer, *Maria Montessori*, 328.

32. Montessori, et al., *The Child in the Church*, 23.

33. Kramer, *Maria Montessori*, 251.

34. Maria Montessori, *The Absorbent Mind*, trans. Claude A. Claremont (New York: Dell Publishing Co., 1967), 108–126.

35. Montessori, *The Absorbent Mind*, 290.

36. Kramer, *Maria Montessori*, 367.

37. Montessori, *Discovery of the Child*, 9.

38. Montessori, *Discovery of the Child*, 326.

39. Maccheroni came from a family interested in education. Her father began a Froebelian *kindergarten* in the Maccheroni home and developed a training college for teachers.

40. Phyllis Wallbank, interview by her daughter Judith, November 2009, Montessori Memoirs, Wallbank Educational Trust, accessed February 14, 2013, *http://pwet.org.uk/montessori.shtml*.

41. Kramer, *Maria Montessori*, 351.

42. Kramer, *Maria Montessori*, 275.

43. Claremont, an engineer, was a leader in England and the United States, conducting training courses with his wife, Francesca. He translated Montessori's *The Absorbent Mind*. Joosten's mother helped found the movement in Holland, but he spent much of his life training Montessorians in India and Sri Lanka. In 1973 Joosten was appointed director of the Montessori Training Center of Minnesota, making it the official AMI training center in the U.S. Standing will be commented on later in the chapter.

44. Povell, *Montessori Comes to America*, 67.

45. Dorothy M. Gaudiose, *Mary's House: Mary Pyle Under the Spiritual Guidance of Padre Pio* (New York: Alba House, 1993), 27–30.

46. Kramer, *Maria Montessori*, 275.

47. These photographs can be found in the collection of the E. M. Standing Center at Seattle University, Seattle, WA.

48. Standing, *Maria Monessori*, 85.

49. The back cover of the 1962 edition of Standing's biography of Montessori says that Standing "became a Catholic in 1923." This is a traditional date, acknowledged by the E. M. Standing Center at Seattle University, but no discussion or evidence has been found as yet to verify this. E. Mortimer Standing, *Maria Montessori: Her Life and Work* (New York: New American Library, 1962), back cover.

50. Standing, *Maria Montessori*, 69.

51. Standing, *Maria Montessori*, 88.

52. E. M. Standing, *Montessori Revolution in Education* (New York: Schocken Books, 1971), 42.

53. Standing, *Montessori Revolution*, 17.

54. Standing, *Montessori Revolution*, 202. This idea refers to Montessori's first chapter in *The Child in the Church*, 7.

55. Montessori, et al., *The Child in the Church*, 110.

56. Phyllis Wallbank, interview by her daughter Judith, November 2009, Montessori Memoirs, Wallbank Educational Trust, accessed February 14, 2013, *http://pwet.org.uk/montessori.shtml*.

Chapter 3

1. Philip Sheldrake, *A Brief History of Spirituality* (Oxford: Blackwell Publishing, 2011), 11.

2. I visited Sophia in Rome about five times, either with family or alone.

3. Eugenio Zolli, *Before the Dawn: Autobiographical Reflections by Eugenio Zolli Former Chief Rabbi of Rome* (San Francisco: Ignatius Press, 2008), 25.

4. Zolli was born Israel Zoller, and became the chief rabbi of Rome in 1938. On his mother's side of the family there had been rabbis and scholars for over two centuries. On February 13, 1945, Zolli was

baptized with his family and took the name Eugenio Maria. The new name paid homage to the reigning pontiff, Pius XII, who had been quietly generous to the Jewish community through Zolli during the German occupation.

For additional information about Zolli and reactions to his conversion see Wallace P. Sillanpoa and Robert G. Weisbord, "The Baptized Rabbi of Rome: The Zolli Case," *Judaism* 38, no. 1 (Winter 1989): 74–91; and Wallace P. Sillanpoa and Robert G. Weisbord, "The Zolli Conversion: Background and Motives," *Judaism* 38, no. 2 (Spring 1989): 203–215. For a general account of the Roman Ghetto and Jewish persecution elsewhere in Italy see Alexander Stille, *Benevolence and Betrayal: Five Italian Jewish Families under Fascism* (New York: Summit Books, 1991).

5. Jerome W. Berryman, "The Work of Sofia Cavalletti: A Bibliography and Brief Introduction," *Constructive Triangle* 5, no. 1 (Winter 1978): 36.

6. Scottie May, "Sofia Cavalletti," Christian Educators of the 20th Century Project, Talbot School of Theology, accessed February 14, 2013, *http://www2.Talbot.edu/ce20/educators/view.cfm=sofia_cavalletti.*

7. Sofia Cavalletti, *The Religious Potential of the Child: Experiencing Scripture and Liturgy with Young Children* (Chicago, IL: Liturgy Training Publications, 1992).

8. This story has slightly different versions. See Maria Montessori, et al., *The Child in the Church*, 131; Sofia Cavalletti and Gianna Gobbi, *Teaching Doctrine and Liturgy: The Montessori Approach*, trans. Sister M. Juliana, O.P (New York: Alba House, 1966), 31; and Cavalletti, *Religious Potential*, 40. What the versions have in common is the joyful response of the children when Sofia opened the Bible and talked seriously with them about God. This was so deeply satisfying to her that she devoted the rest of her life to understanding and nourishing the religious potential of children, while continuing as a biblical scholar.

9. Tina Lillig, ed. *Catechesis of the Good Shepherd: Essential Realities* (Chicago: Catechesis of the Good Shepherd, 2004), 112.

10. Gianna Gobbi, *Listening To God with Children: The Montessori Method Applied to the Catechesis of Children*, trans. and ed. Rebekah Rojcewicz (Loveland, OH: Treehaus, 1998), 63–70.

11. Guiseppe Alberigo, *A Brief History of Vatican II* (Maryknoll, NY: Orbis, 2006), 1.

12. Montessori, et al., *The Child in the Church*, 132.

13. Sofia Cavalletti and Gianna Gobbi, *Io sono il buon Pastore*, 5 vols. (Rome: Ufficio Catechistico di Roma, 1970–71). A 2006–2009 edition of this work, published by Tau, can be found on *Amazon.com*.

14. Cavalletti, *The Religious Potential of the Child*, 161.

15. Cavalletti, *The Religious Potential of the Child*, 164.

16. Standing, *Montessori Revolution*, 15.

17. Montessori, et al., *The Child in the Church*, 132.

18. Discussion of the changing views of salvation history and related matters draws heavily on Mary C. Boys, *Biblical Interpretation in Religious Education: A Study of the Kerygmatic Era* (Birmingham, AL: Religious Education Press, 1980), 81–82.

19. Lillig, *Catechesis of the Good Shepherd,* xi. This book is also important because of the collection of pictures as well as memoirs. One picture, entitled simply "Gianna, Silvana, Sofia, and Tilde," includes four key leaders from the early days of the Center in Rome (72).

20. Cavalletti, *The Religious Potential of the Child*, 45.

21. Jerome W. Berryman, "The Chaplain's Strange Language: A Unique Contribution to the Health Care Team." In *Life, Faith, Hope & Magic: The Chaplaincy in Pediatric Cancer Care*, ed. Jan van Eys and Edward J. Mahnke (Houston: University of Texas System Cancer Center, 1985), 15–39.

22. Jerome W. Berryman, *Godly Play: An Imaginative Approach to Religious Education* (Minneapolis, MN: Augsburg, 1995), 77.

23. Samuel Terrien, *The Elusive Presence: Toward a New Biblical Theology* (Eugene, OR: Wipf and Stock, 2000), 63–66.

Chapter 4

1. T. S. Eliot, "The Four Quartets: Burnt Norton," in *The Complete Poems and Plays 1909–1950* (New York: Harcourt, Brace, 1952), 119, 122.

2. Standing, *Montessori Revolution*, 64–65.

3. D. W. Winnicott, *Playing and Reality* (London: Tavistock Publications, 1985), 5.

4. John Macquarrie, *Principles of Christian Theology*, 2nd ed. (New York: Scribner & Sons, 1977), 106.

5. Karl Rahner, *Further Theology of the Spiritual Life 2*. Vol. 8 of *Theological Investigations* (London: Darton, Longman & Todd, 1971) 39–40.

6. Hans Urs von Balthasar, *Unless You Become Like this Child*, trans. by Erasmo Leiva-Merikakis (San Francisco: Ignatius Press, 1991), 19.

7. David L. Schindler, ed., *Hans Urs von Balthasar: His Life and Work* (San Francisco: Ignatius Press, 1991), 3.

8. Margery Williams, *The Velveteen Rabbit, or, How Toys Become Real* (New York: Random House, 1986), 14–15.

9. Nikki Bado-Fralick and Rebecca Sachs Norris, *Toying with God: The World of Religious Games and Dolls* (Waco, TX: Baylor University Press, 2010), 53.

10. Bado-Fralick and Norris, *Toying with God*, 150–155.

11. Berryman, *The Complete Guide To Godly Play*, vol. 2, 73–80.

12. Dorothy L. Sayers, *The Mind of the Maker* (London: Mowbray, 1994), 21.

13. Sayers, *The Mind of the Maker*, 172–173.

14. This agenda was set in part by D. Campbell Wyckoff, who was Loder's professor and mentor at Princeton, as well as my own. Wyckoff was working on his *Theory and Design of Christian Education* when they first met. Wyckoff's book stressed the need for one clear objective "intended as a guide for the whole education process." D. Campbell Wyckoff, *Theory and Design of Christian Education Curriculum* (Philadelphia: Westminster, 1961), 62. Wyckoff argued that theology provides both the content for Christian education and is "a source of insight and direction in determining the context, scope, purpose, process, and design of curriculum," 94. He also cautioned that the behavioral sciences should not be neglected. Loder embraced the behavioral sciences and physics in his bridge-building between religion and science. His key organizing thought, the "transformational moment," was the bridge.

15. James E. Loder, *The Transforming Moment: Understanding Convictional Experiences*, 2nd ed. (Colorado Springs, CO: Helmers & Howard, 1989), 72.

16. Loder, *The Transforming Moment*, 80.

17. Loder, *The Transforming Moment*, 80–81.

18. Loder, *The Transforming Moment*, 87.

19. Loder, *The Transforming Moment*, 115–116.

20. Gabriel Marcel, *Creative Fidelity*, trans. Robert Rosenthal (New York: Fordham University Press, 2002), 172. Marcel preferred the term "permeability," arguing that "participation" was too ambiguous. When "permeable," the boundary of the self becomes open to experiencing both what is beyond and what is within, similar to the function of the middle realm.

21. Irvin D. Yalom, *Existential Psychotherapy* (New York: Basic Books, 1980), 8–9.

22. Berryman, "The Parable of the Good Shepherd" in *The Complete Guide To Godly Play*, vol. 3, 77–86.

23. As a student of Freud, Loder began his study of the creative process with the work of Herbert Silberer (1882–1923), a Viennese psychoanalyst, whose work strayed from Freudian orthodoxy toward Jungian themes, such as the occult and alchemy, to the extent that he was rejected by the inner circle and hanged himself. However, he wrote an important article in 1909 about the hypnagogic state, the state of consciousness between waking and sleeping. Loder does not mention Silberer in *The Transforming Moment*, but he relied on him almost exclusively in *Religious Pathology and Christian Faith* to develop his view of the creative process.

24. R. Keith Sawyer, *Explaining Creativity: The Science of Human Innovation* (Oxford: Oxford University Press, 2012), 15–34.

25. James E. Loder, *Religious Pathology and Christian Faith* (Philadelphia, PA: Westminster Press, 1966), 178.

26. James E. Loder, "Transformation in Christian Education," *The Princeton Seminary Bulletin* 3, no.1 (1980): 11–15.

27. James E. Loder, *The Transforming Moment: Understanding Convictional Experiences*, 2nd ed. (Colorado Springs, CO: Helmers & Howard, 1989), 40.

28. Jerome W. Berryman, *Godly Play: An Imaginative Approach to Religious Education* (Minneapolis, MN: Augsburg, 1995), 93–135, especially 102, 150; Jerome W. Berryman, *Teaching Godly Play: How to Mentor the Spiritual Development of Children.* 2nd ed. (Denver,

CO: Morehouse Education Resources, 2009), 116–128 and 136–137; and Jerome W. Berryman, *Children and the Theologians: Clearing the Way for Grace* (New York: Morehouse, 2009), 230–244.

29. Loder, *The Transforming Moment*, 204.

30. Jonah Lehrer, *Imagine: How Creativity Works* (New York: Houghton Mifflin Harcourt, 2012), 17.

31. Lehrer, *Imagine*, 30.

32. Howard Gardner, *Frames of Mind: The Theory of Multiple Intelligences* (New York: Basic Books, 2011), xxi.

33. Howard Gardner, *Creating Minds: An Anatomy of Creativity Seen Through the Lives of Freud, Einstein, Picasso, Stravinsky, Eliot, Graham, and Gandhi* (New York: Basic Books, 2011), xiii–xiv.

34. Mihaly Csikszentmihalyi and Isabella Selega Csikszentmihalyi, eds., *Optimal Experience: Psychological Studies of Flow in Consciousness* (Cambridge: Cambridge University Press, 1995), 92–117.

35. Dan Ariely, *The (Honest) Truth About Dishonesty: How We Lie to Everyone—Especially Ourselves* (New York: Harper, 2012), 163–189.

36. Loder, *The Transforming Moment*, 209–210.

37. Loder, *Religious Pathology and Christian Faith*, 128.

Chapter 5

1. W. B. Yeats, "The Second Coming," *The Collected Poems of W. B. Yeats*, ed. Richard J. Finneran (New York: CollierBooks, 1989) 187.

2. Richard Ellmann, *Yeats: The Man and the Masks* (New York: E. P. Dutton & Co., Inc.), 285.

3. T. S. Eliot, "The Four Quartets: Little Gidding," in *The Complete Poems and Plays: 1909–1950*, 144–145.

4. Mihaly Csikszentmihalyi, *Beyond Boredom and Anxiety: The Experience of Play in Work and Games* (San Francisco: Jossey-Bass Publishers, 1975), 35–54.

5. Mihaly Csikszentmihalyi, *Flow: The Psychology of Optimal Experience* (New York: Harper Perennial, 1990), 43–70.

6. Loder, *The Transforming Moment*, 18–26. Loder appears to stress justification and regeneration, which are acts of God alone, to the

detriment of sanctification, which involves the person's involvement as well as God's grace. In my view Loder has a better balance
between these two theological doctrines than is sometimes seen. The
"Holy Spirit converges with the Eucharist (114)" and there is a "sanc-
tifying unity" with Christ (115). He also talked about "doing something about one's convictional experience (194)" in the "sacramental
community (196)." In addition he emphasized at times "continuity,"
"process," "human agents" and being involved in the Christian life
(208–209).

7. Harvey Whitehouse and Luther H. Martin, eds., *Theorizing Religions Past: Archeology, History, and Cognition* (Walnut Creek, CA:
AltaMira Press, 2004), 11, 205.

8. Mihaly Csikszentmihalyi and Isabella Selega Csikszentmihalyi, eds.,
Optimal Experience: Psychological Studies of Flow in Consciousness,
10–11.

9. Mihaly Csikszentmihalyi, *The Evolving Self: A Psychology for the
Third Millennium* (New York: Harper Perenial, 1993), 197–199.

10. Howard Gardner, *Creating Minds: An Anatomy of Creativity Seen
Through the Lives of Freud, Einstein, Picasso, Stravinsky, Eliot, Graham,
and Gandhi* (New York: Basic Books, 1993), 37.

11. Mihaly Csikszentmihalyi, *Creativity: Flow and the Psychology of
Discovery and Invention* (New York: HarperCollins, 1996).

Creativity's social dimension has three centers of influence. The
first for Csikszentmihalyi is "the domain," where "a set of symbolic
rules and procedures" reside. In Gardner's terminology this is "the
work." It includes the relevant symbol system of the domain in which
the creative individual is working.

A second center is "the field," which for Csikszentmihalyi includes
"all the individuals who act as gatekeepers to the domain." For Gardner this part of the creative process is called "other persons." They are
family and peers in the early years. This group later expands to rivals,
judges, and supporters (Gardner 1993, 9). An idea, which is personally
novel, becomes socially significant through the interaction among individuals, domains, and fields (Gardner 1993, 36).

The third center of activity is "the person," who works in a particular domain (or sets up a new domain) and moves beyond personal creativity into being creative socially when the field accepts the new idea

(Csikszentmihalyi 1996, 27–28). Gardner notes that a creative person "solves problems, fashions products, or defines new questions in a domain in a way that is initially considered novel but that ultimately becomes accepted in a particular cultural setting" (Gardner 1993, 35).

12. Lehrer, *Imagine*, 139.

13. Catherine Garvey, *Play: The Developing Child,* 2nd ed. (Cambridge, MA: Harvard University Press,1990), 5.

14. Anthony D. Pellegrini, *The Role of Play in Human Development* (Oxford: Oxford University Press, 2009), 21.

15. Thomas Lewis, Fari Amini, and Richard Lannon, *A General Theory of Love* (New York: Random House, 2000), 63.

16. Daniel Goleman, *Emotional Intelligence* (New York: Bantam, 2005), 80–83.

17. The biological grounding of love incorporates the whole chorus of our affective systems. The study of the ancient parts of our brain is an expanding field, as demonstrated by such books as Jaak Panksepp's *Affective Neuroscience: The Foundations of Human and Animal Emotions* (Oxford: Oxford University Press), and his book with Lucy Biven referred to in the text, *The Archeaeology of the Mind: Neuroevolutionary Origins of Human Emotions* (New York: W. W. Norton, 2012).

18. Quoted without a source in Lewis, Amini, and Lannon 2000, 34.

19. Philip Sheldrake, *A Brief History of Spirituality* (Oxford: Blackwell, 2011), 3.

20. Sheldrake, *Brief History of Sprituality*, 2–3.

21. Dante Alighieri, *The Divine Comedy: Paradiso, Volume III, Part I*, trans. Charles S. Singleton (Princeton, NJ: Princeton University Press, 1991), 115.

22. Sheldrake, *Brief History of Spirituality*, 77.

23. Richard of St. Victor. *The Twelve Patriarchs; The Mystical Ark; Book Three of the Trinity*, trans. Grover A. Zinn (New York: Paulist Press, 1979), 157.

24. E. M. Standing, *Maria Montessori: Her Life and Work* (New York: Plume, 1984), 178.

25. Gabriel Marcel, *Creative Fidelity,* trans. Robert Rosenthal (New York: Fordham University Press, 2002), 163.

26. Marcel, *Creative Fidelity,* 164.

27. Marcel, *Creative Fidelity,* 167.

28. Marcel, *Creative Fidelity,* 168.

29. Marcel, *Creative Fidelity,* 168.

30. R. Keith Sawyer, Vera John-Steiner, Seana Moran, Robert J. Sternberg, David Henry Feldman, Jeanne Nakamura, and Mihaly Csikszentmihalyi, *Creativity and Development* (Oxford: Oxford Univesity Press, 2003), 12–60.

31. James W. Fowler, *Stages of Faith: The Psychology of Human Development and the Quest for Meaning* (San Francisco: HarperSanFrancisco, 1981), 315–316.

32. Jim Fowler and Sam Keen with Jerome Berryman, ed., *Life Maps: The Journey of Human Faith* (Waco, TX: Word Books Publisher, 1978), 91–95.

Chapter 6

1. Jerome W. Berryman, *Godly Play: An Imaginative Approach to Religious Education* (Minneapolis, MN: Augsburg, 1995); Jerome W. Berryman, *Teaching Godly Play: How to Mentor the Spiritual Development of Children,* 2nd ed. (Denver, CO: Morehouse Education Resources, 2009); Jerome W. Berryman, *Children and the Theologians: Clearing the Way for Grace* (New York: Morehouse, 2009).

2. John M. Hull, "A Gift to the Child: A New Pedagogy for Teaching Religion to Young Children" in *Religious Education* 91(Winter 1996), 172–188.

3. Berryman, *The Complete Guide To Godly Play,* vol. 4, 32–68.

4. David Hay with Rebecca Nye, *The Spirit of the Child,* rev. ed. (London: Jessica Kinsley, 2006), 92–128. An overview diagram is at page 114.

5. Andrew D. Lester, *Pastoral Care with Children in Crisis* (Philadelphia: Westminster Press, 1985), 23–35 (concerning the neglect of the child in pastoral care) and 85–133 (concerning methods for care).

6. Andrew D. Lester, *When Children Suffer* (Philadelphia: Westminster Press, 1987), 69–172.

7. This booklet, based on the Finnish book *Kohti leikkivää kirkkoa*, ed. Kalevi Virtanen and published by the Finnish Evangelical Lutheran Parishes's Centre for Child Work, Helsinki, Finland 2006, is available online, accessed online May 30, 2013, *http://www.evl-slk.fi/ files/40/ Church_20at_20play_20netti.pdf.*

8. Berryman, *Complete Guide To Godly Play,* vol. 8, 156–160.

9. Sheldrake, *A Brief History of Spirituality*, xiii.

10. Sheldrake, *A Brief History of Spirituality*, 204.

11. Sheldrake, *A Brief History of Spirituality*, 208–209.

12. Charles Dickens, *A Christmas Carol* (Oxford: Benediction Classics, 2012), 151.

bibliography

Alberigo, Guiseppe. *A Brief History of Vatican II*. Maryknoll, NY: Orbis, 2006.

Ariely, Dan. *The (Honest) Truth About Dishonesty: How We Lie to Everyone—Especially Ourselves*. New York: Harper, 2012.

Babini, Valeria P., and Luisa Lama. *Una "Donna Nuova": Il feminismo scientifico di Maria Montessori*. Milan: FrancoAngeli, 2003.

Bado-Fralick, Nikki, and Rebecca Sachs Norris. *Toying with God: The World of Religious Games and Dolls*. Waco, TX: Baylor University Press, 2010.

Balthasar, Hans Urs von. *The Realm of Metaphysics in the Modern Age*. Vol. 5 of *The Glory of the Lord: A Theological Aesthetics*. Edited by Brian McNeil and John Riches. Translated by Oliver Davies, Andrew Louth, Brian McNeil, John Saward, and Rowan Williams. San Francisco: Ignatius Press, 1991.

Balthasar, Hans Urs von. *Unless You Become Like This Child*. Translated by Erasmo Leiva-Merikakis. San Francisco: Ignatius Press, 1991.

Balthasar, Hans Urs von. *Presence and Thought: An Essay on the Religious Philosophy of Gregory of Nyssa*. Translated by Mark Sebanc. San Francisco: Ignatius Press, 1995.

Bass, Diana Butler. *Christianity After Religion: The End of Church and the Birth of a New Spiritual Awakening*. New York: HarperCollins, 2012.

Bates, Dennis, Gloria Durka, and Friedrich Schweitzer, eds. *Education, Religion and Society: Essays in honour of John M. Hull.* London: Routledge, 2006.

Beckoff, Marc. *Animals at Play: Rules of the Game.* Philadelphia: Temple University Press, 2008.

Berryman, Jerome W. "The Work of Sofia Cavalletti: A Bibliography and Brief Introduction." *Constructive Triangle* 5, no. 1 (Winter 1978): 32–45.

Berryman, Jerome W. "The Chaplain's Strange Language: A Unique Contribution to the Health Care Team." In *Life, Faith, Hope & Magic: The Chaplaincy in Pediatric Cancer Care,* edited by Jan van Eys and Edward J. Mahnke, 15–39. Houston: University of Texas System Cancer Center, 1985.

Berryman, Jerome W. "Teaching As Presence and the Existential Curriculum." *Religious Education* 85, no. 4 (Fall 1990): 509–534.

Berryman, Jerome W. *Godly Play: An Imaginative Approach to Religious Education.* Minneapolis, MN: Augsburg, 1995.

Berryman, Jerome W. *Teaching Godly Play: How to Mentor the Spiritual Development of Children.* 2nd ed. Denver, CO: Morehouse Education Resources, 2009.

Berryman, Jerome W. *Children and the Theologians: Clearing the Way for Grace.* New York: Morehouse, 2009.

Bruner, Jerome S. *Beyond the Information Given: Studies in the Psychology of Knowing.* Edited by Jeremy M. Anglin. New York: W. W. Norton, 1973.

Boys, Mary C. *Biblical Interpretation in Religious Education: A Study of the Kerygmatic Era.* Birmingham, AL: Religious Education Press, 1980.

Buckenmeyer, Robert G. *The California Lectures of Maria Montessori, 1915: Collected Speeches and Writings.* Vol. 15 of *The Clio Montessori Series.* Oxford: Clio Press, 1997.

Bunge, Marcia J., ed. *The Child in the Bible.* With the assistance of Terrence E. Fretheim and Beverly Roberts Gaventa. Grand Rapids, MI: Wm. B. Eerdmans, 2008.

Bushnell, Horace. *Christian Nurture.* Grand Rapids, MI: Baker Book House, 1979.

Cassirer, Ernst. *Kant's Life and Thought*. Translated by James Haden. New Haven, CT: Yale University Press, 1981.

Cavalletti, Sofia. *The Religious Potential of the Child: Experiencing Scripture and Liturgy with Young Children*. Translated by Patricia M. Coulter and Julie M. Coulter. Chicago, IL: Liturgy Training Publications, 1992.

Cavalletti, Sofia. *History's Golden Thread: The History of Salvation*. Translated by Rebekah Rojcewicz. Chicago: Catechesis of the Good Shepherd, 1999.

Cavalletti, Sofia. *Living Liturgy: Elementary Reflections*. Translated by Patricia M. Coulter and Julie Coulter-English. Oak Park, IL: Catechesis of the Good Shepherd, 1998.

Cavalletti, Sofia and Gianna Gobbi. *Teaching Doctrine and Liturgy: The Montessori Approach*. Translated by Sister M. Juliana, O.P. New York: Alba House, 1966.

Chattin-McNichols, John. *The Montessori Controversy*. Albany, NY: Delmar, 1992.

Csikszentmihalyi, Mihaly. *Beyond Boredom and Anxiety: The Experience of Play in Work and Games*. San Francisco: Jossey-Bass, 1975.

Csikszentmihalyi, Mihaly. *Flow: The Psychology of Optimal Experience*. New York: Harper Perennial, 1990.

Csikszentmihalyi, Mihaly. *The Evolving Self: A Psychology for the Third Millennium*. New York: Harper Perennial, 1993.

Csikszentmihalyi, Mihaly. *Creativity: Flow and the Psychology of Discovery and Invention*. New York: HarperCollins, 1996.

Csikszentmihalyi, Mihaly and Isabella Selega Csikszentmihalyi, eds. *Optimal Experience: Psychological Studies of Flow in Consciousness*. Cambridge: Cambridge University Press, 1995.

Cunningham, Hugh. *The Invention of Childhood*. London: BBC Books, 2006.

Davis, Caroline Franks. *The Evidential Force of Religious Experience*. Oxford: Oxford University Press, 1989.

Elias, John L. *A History of Christian Education: Protestant, Catholic, and Orthodox Perspectives*. Malabar, FL: Krieger, 2002.

Eliot, T. S. *The Complete Poems and Plays 1909–1950*. New York: Harcourt, Brace, 1952.

Ellmann, Richard. *Yeats: The Man and the Masks*. New York: E. P. Dutton & Co., Inc., 1948.

Engelmann, Kim V. *Running in Circles: How False Spirituality Traps Us in Unhealthy Relationships*. Downer's Grove, IL: InterVarsity Press, 2007.

Fauconnier, Gilles and Mark Turner. *The Way We Think: Conceptual Blending and the Mind's Hidden Complexities*. New York: Basic Books, 2002.

Fowler, James W. *Stages of Faith: The Psychology of Development and the Quest for Meaning*. San Francisco: Harper and Row, 1981.

Fowler, Jim and Sam Keen. *Life Maps: Conversations on the Journey of Faith*. Edited by Jerome W. Berryman. Waco, TX: Word Books, 1978.

Gardner, Howard. *Frames of Mind: The Theory of Multiple Intelligences*. New York: Basic Books, 2011.

Gardner, Howard. *Creating Minds: An Anatomy of Creativity Seen Through the Lives of Freud, Einstein, Picasso, Stravinsky, Eliot, Graham, and Gandhi*. New York: Basic Books, 1993.

Gardner, Howard. *Intelligence Reframed: Multiple Intelligences for the 21st Century*. New York: Basic Books, 1999.

Garvey, Catherine. *Play: The Developing Child*. 2nd ed. Cambridge, MA: Harvard University Press, 1990.

Gaudiose, Dorothy M. *Mary's House: Mary Pyle: Under the Spiritual Guidance of Padre Pio*. New York: Alba House, 1993.

Gobbi, Gianna. *Listening to God with Children: The Montessori Method Applied to the Catechesis of Children*. Translated and edited by Rebekah Rojcewicz. Loveland, OH: Treehaus, 1998.

Goleman, Daniel. *Emotional Intelligence*. New York: Bantam, 2005.

Grazzini, Massimo. *Bibliografia Montessori*. Brescia, Italy: La Scuola editrice, 1965.

Hay, David, with Rebecca Nye. *The Spirit of the Child*. Rev. ed. London: Jessica Kingsley, 2006.

Herzog, Kristin. *Children and Our Global Future: Theological and Social Challenges*. Cleveland, OH: Pilgrim Press, 2005.

Himes, Andrew. *The Sword of the Lord: The Roots of Fundamentalism in an American Family*. Seattle, WA: Chiara Press, 2011.

Holmes, III, Urban T. *A History of Christian Spirituality: An Analytical Introduction*. Harrisburg, PA: Morehouse, 2002.

Huizinga, Johan. *Homo Ludens: A Study of the Play Element in Culture*. Boston, MA: Beacon Press, 1955.

Jaspers, Karl. *Philosophy of Existence*. Translated by Richard F. Grabay. Philadelphia: University of Pennsylvania Press, 1995.

Keen, Sam. *Apology for Wonder*. New York: Harper & Row, 1969.

Keen, Sam. *Gabriel Marcel*. Richmond, VA: John Knox Press, 1967.

Kramer, Rita. *Maria Montessori: A Biography*. With Foreword by Anna Freud. Reading, MA: Addison Wesley, 1988.

Lehrer, Jonah. *Imagine: How Creativity Works*. Boston: Houghton Mifflin Harcourt, 2012.

Lester, Andrew D. *Pastoral Care with Children in Crisis*. Philadelphia: Westminster Press, 1985.

Lester, Andrew D. *When Children Suffer: A Sourcebook for Ministry with Children in Crisis*. Philadelphia: Westminster Press, 1987.

Lewis, Thomas, Fari Amini, and Richard Lannon. *A General Theory of Love*. New York: Random House, 2000.

Lillig, Tina, ed. *Catechesis of the Good Shepherd: Essential Realities*. Chicago: Catechesis of the Good Shepherd, 2004.

Loder, James E. *Religious Pathology and Christian Faith*. Philadelphia: Westminster Press, 1966.

Loder, James E. "Transformation in Christian Education." *The Princeton Seminary Bulletin* 3, no.1 (1980): 11–15.

Loder, James E. *The Transforming Moment: Understanding Convictional Experiences*. 2nd ed. Colorado Springs, CO: Helmers & Howard, 1989.

Loder, James E. and James W. Fowler. "Conversations on Fowler's *Stages of Faith* and Loder's *The Transforming Moment*." *Religious Education* 77, no. 2, (1982): 133–148.

Loder, James E. and W. Jim Neidhardt. *The Knight's Move: The Relational Logic of the Spirit in Theology and Science*. Colorado Springs, CO: Helmers & Howard, 1992.

Maccheroni, Anna M. *A True Romance: Doctor Maria Montessori as I Knew Her*. Edinburgh: Darien Press, 1947.

Macquarrie, John. *Principles of Christian Theology*. 2nd ed. New York: Scribner & Sons, 1977.

Marcel, Gabriel. *Reflection and Mystery*. Vol. 1 of *The Mystery of Being*. Chicago: Gateway, 1960.

Marcel, Gabriel. *Creative Fidelity*. Translated by Robert Rosenthal. New York: Fordham University Press, 2002.

Marcel, Gabriel. *The Philosophy of Existentialism*. New York: Citadel Press, 2002.

May, Rollo. *The Discovery of Being: Writings in Existential Psychology*. New York: W. W. Norton, 1983.

McBrien, Richard P. *Catholicism: Study Edition*. San Francisco: Harper SanFrancisco, 1981.

Mithen, Steven. *The Prehistory of the Mind: A Search for the Origins of Art, Religion and Science*. London: Phoenix, 1996.

Montessori, Maria, and others. *The Child in the Church*. Edited by E. M. Standing. St. Paul, MN: Catechetical Guild, 1965.

Montessori, Maria. *Spontaneous Activity in Education*. Translated by Florence Simmonds. New York: Schocken Books, 1969.

Montessori, Maria. *The Absorbent Mind*. Translated by Claude A. Claremont. New York: Delta, 1967.

Montessori, Maria. *The Discovery of the Child*. Translated by M. Joseph Costelloe. Notre Dame, IN: Fides, 1967.

Montessori, Maria. *The Montessori Method*. Translated by Anne E. George. New York: Schocken Books, 1970.

Moran, Gabriel. *Showing How: The Act of Teaching*. Valley Forge, PA: Trinity Press International, 1997.

Nelson, Claudia. *Precocious Children & Childish Adults: Age Inversion in Victorian Literature*. Baltimore, MD: Johns Hopkins University Press, 2012.

Newberry, Josephine. *Church Kindergarten Resource Book*. Rev. ed. Atlanta, GA: John Knox, 1976.

Otto, Rudolf. *The Idea of the Holy*. 2nd ed. Oxford: Oxford University Press, 1950.

Panksepp, Jaak. *Affective Neuroscience: The Foundations of Human and Animal Emotions*. Oxford: Oxford University Press, 1998.

Panksepp, Jaak and Lucy Biven. *The Archeology of Mind: Neuro-evolutionary Origins of Human Emotions*. New York: W. W. Norton, 2012.

Parkhurst, Helen. *Education on the Dalton Plan*. New York: E. P. Dutton, 1929.

Pellegrini, Anthony D. *The Role of Play in Human Development*. Oxford: Oxford University Press, 2009.

Phillips, J. B. *Your God is Too Small*. New York: Touchstone Books, 2004.

Plesk, Paul E. *Creativity, Innovation, and Quality*. Milwaukee, WI: ASQ Quality Press, 1997.

Polyani, Michael and Harry Prosch. *Meaning*. Chicago: University of Chicago Press, 1975.

Povell, Phyllis. *Montessori Comes to America: The Leadership of Maria Montessori and Nancy McCormick Rambusch*. Lanham, MD: University Press of America, 2010.

Rahner, Karl. *Further Theology of the Spiritual Life 2*. Vol. 8 of *Theological Investigations*. London: Darton, Longman & Todd, 1971.

Reed, James E. and Ronnie Prevost. *A History of Christian Education*. Nashville, TN: Broadman & Holman, 1993.

Richard of St. Victor. *The Twelve Patriarchs; The Mystical Ark; Book Three of the Trinity*. Translated with Introduction by Grover A. Zinn. The Classics of Western Spirituality. New York: Paulist Press, 1979.

Robinson, Edward. *The Original Vision: A Study of the Religious Experience of Childhood*. New York: Seabury, 1983.

Robinson, Marilynne. *When I Was a Child I Read Books: Essays*. New York: Farrar, Strauss and Giroux, 2012.

Sawyer, R. Keith. *Explaining Creativity: The Science of Human Innovation*. 2nd ed. Oxford: Oxford University Press, 2012.

Sawyer, R. Keith, Vera John-Steiner, Seana Moran, Robert J. Sternberg, David Henry Feldman, Jeanne Nakamura, and Mihaly Csikszentmihalyi. *Creativity and Development*. Oxford: Oxford University Press, 2003.

Sayers, Dorothy. *The Mind of the Maker*. London: Mowbray, 1994.

Schindler, David L., ed. *Hans Urs von Balthasar: His Life and Work*. San Francisco: Ignatius Press, 1991.

Sheldrake, Philip. *A Brief History of Spirituality*. Oxford: Blackwell, 2011.

Sillanpoa, Wallace P. and Robert G. Weisbord, "The Baptized Rabbi of Rome: The Zolli Case" *Judaism* 38, no. 1 (Winter 1989): 74–91.

Sillanpoa, Wallace P. and Robert G. Weisbord. "The Zolli Conversion: Background and Motives" *Judaism* 38, no. 2 (Spring 1989): 203–215.

Sobel, Dava. *A More Perfect Heaven: How Copernicus Revolutionized the Cosmos*. New York: Walker, 2011.

Standing, E. M. *Maria Montessori: Her Life and Work*. New York: Plume, 1984.

Standing, E. M. *Montessori Revolution in Education*. New York: Schocken Books, 1971.

Stille, Alexander. *Benevolence and Betrayal: Five Italian Jewish Families under Fascism*. New York: Summit Books, 1991.

Terrien, Samuel. *The Elusive Presence: Toward a New Biblical Theology*. Eugene, OR: Wipf & Stock, 2000.

Thomas, R. S. *Collected Poems 1945–1990*. London: Phoenix, 2000.

Thomas, R. S. *Collected Later Poems 1988–2000*. Northumberland, UK: Bloodaxe, 2004.

Tracy, David. *Blessed Rage for Order: The New Pluralism in Theology*. New York: Seabury Press, 1978.

Walsh, James, ed. *The Cloud of Unknowing*. The Classics of Western Spirituality. New York: Paulist Press, 1981

Watts, Fraser, Rebecca Nye, and Sara Savage. *Psychology for Christian Ministry*. London: Routledge, 2002.

Westerhoff, III, John H. *Will Our Children Have Faith?* 3rd ed. New York: Morehouse, 2012.

Westerhoff, III, John H. and O. C. Edwards, Jr., eds. *A Faithful Church: Issues in the History of Catechesis*. Wilton, CT: Morehouse-Barlow, 1981.

Whitehouse, Harvey and Luther H. Martin, eds. *Theorizing Religions Past: Archeology, History, and Cognition*. Walnut Creek, CA: Altamira Press, 2004.

Williams, Margery. *The Velveteen Rabbit, or, How Toys Become Real.* New York: Random House, 1986.

Winnicott, D. W. *Playing and Reality.* London: Tavistock Publications, 1985.

Wyckoff, D. Campbell. *Theory and Design of Christian Education Curriculum.* Philadelphia: Westminster Press, 1961.

Yalom, Irvin D. *Existential Psychotherapy.* New York: Basic Books, 1980.

Yeats, W. B. *The Collected Poems of W. B. Yeats.* Edited by Richard J. Finneran. New ed. York: CollierBooks, 1989.

Zolli, Eugenio. *Before the Dawn: Autobiographical Reflections by Eugenio Zolli Former Chief Rabbi of Rome.* San Francisco: Ignatius Press, 2008.

index